FOREWORD

The collection of "Everything Will Be Okay" travel phrasebooks published by T&P Books is designed for people traveling abroad for tourism and business. The phrasebooks contain what matters most - the essentials for basic communication. This is an indispensable set of phrases to "survive" while abroad.

This phrasebook will help you in most cases where you need to ask something, get directions, find out how much something costs, etc. It can also resolve difficult communication situations where gestures just won't help.

This book contains a lot of phrases that have been grouped according to the most relevant topics. A separate section of the book also provides a small dictionary with more than 1,500 important and useful words.

Take "Everything Will Be Okay" phrasebook with you on the road and you'll have an irreplaceable traveling companion who will help you find your way out of any situation and teach you to not fear speaking with foreigners.

TABLE OF CONTENTS

T&P Books Publishing

Travel phrasebooks collection
«Everything Will Be Okay!»

T&P Books Publishing

PHRASEBOOK

— DUTCH —

THE MOST IMPORTANT PHRASES

This phrasebook contains
the most important
phrases and questions
for basic communication
Everything you need
to survive overseas

By Andrey Taranov

T&p BOOKS

Phrasebook + 1500-word dictionary

English-Dutch phrasebook & concise dictionary

By Andrey Taranov

The collection of "Everything Will Be Okay" travel phrasebooks published by T&P Books is designed for people traveling abroad for tourism and business. The phrasebooks contain what matters most - the essentials for basic communication. This is an indispensable set of phrases to "survive" while abroad.

Another section of the book also provides a small dictionary with more than 1,500 useful words arranged alphabetically. The dictionary includes a lot of gastronomic terms and will be helpful when ordering food at a restaurant or buying groceries at the store.

T&P Books Publishing
www.tpbooks.com

ISBN: 978-1-78492-449-2

This book is also available in E-book formats.
Please visit www.tpbooks.com or the major online bookstores.

PRONUNCIATION

T&P phonetic alphabet	Dutch example	English example
[a]	plasje	shorter than in ask
[â]	kraag	calf, palm
[o], [ɔ]	zondag	drop, baught
[o]	geografie	pod, John
[ō]	oorlog	fall, bomb
[e]	nemen	elm, medal
[ē]	wreed	longer than in bell
[ɛ]	ketterij	man, bad
[ɛ:]	crème	longer than bed, fell
[ə]	tachtig	driver, teacher
[i]	alpinist	shorter than in feet
[ī]	referee	feet, meter
[ʏ]	stadhuis	fuel, tuna
[œ]	druif	German Hölle
[ø]	treurig	eternal, church
[u]	schroef	book
[ʉ]	zuchten	youth, usually
[ū]	minuut	fuel, tuna
[b]	oktober	baby, book
[d]	diepte	day, doctor
[f]	fierheid	face, food
[g]	golfclub	game, gold
[h]	horizon	home, have
[j]	jaar	yes, New York
[k]	klooster	clock, kiss
[l]	politiek	lace, people
[m]	melodie	magic, milk
[n]	netwerk	sang, thing
[p]	peper	pencil, private
[r]	rechter	rice, radio
[s]	smaak	city, boss
[t]	telefoon	tourist, trip
[v]	vijftien	very, river
[w]	waaier	vase, winter

T&P phonetic alphabet	Dutch example	English example
[z]	zacht	zebra, please
[dʒ]	manager	joke, general
[ʃ]	architect	machine, shark
[ŋ]	behang	English, ring
[tʃ]	beertje	church, French
[ʒ]	bougie	forge, pleasure
[x]	acht, gaan	as in Scots 'loch'

LIST OF ABBREVIATIONS

English abbreviations

ab.	-	about
adj	-	adjective
adv	-	adverb
anim.	-	animate
as adj	-	attributive noun used as adjective
e.g.	-	for example
etc.	-	et cetera
fam.	-	familiar
fem.	-	feminine
form.	-	formal
inanim.	-	inanimate
masc.	-	masculine
math	-	mathematics
mil.	-	military
n	-	noun
pl	-	plural
pron.	-	pronoun
sb	-	somebody
sing.	-	singular
sth	-	something
v aux	-	auxiliary verb
vi	-	intransitive verb
vi, vt	-	intransitive, transitive verb
vt	-	transitive verb

Dutch abbreviations

mv.	-	plural

Dutch articles

de	-	common gender
de/het	-	neuter, common gender
het	-	neuter

T&P BOOKS

DUTCH
PHRASEBOOK

This section contains
important phrases that may
come in handy in various
real-life situations.
The phrasebook will help
you ask for directions, clarify
a price, buy tickets, and
order food at a restaurant

T&P Books Publishing

PHRASEBOOK CONTENTS

T&P Books Publishing

The bare minimum

Excuse me, ...	**Pardon, ...** [par'dɔn, ...]
Hello.	**Hallo.** [halɔ]
Thank you.	**Bedankt.** [bə'dankt]
Good bye.	**Tot ziens.** [tɔt zins]
Yes.	**Ja.** [ja]
No.	**Nee.** [nē]
I don't know.	**Ik weet het niet.** [ik wēt ət nit]
Where? | Where to? | When?	**Waar? | Waarheen? | Wanneer?** [wār? | wār'hēn? | wa'nēr?]

I need ...	**Ik heb ... nodig** [ik hɛp ... 'nɔdəx]
I want ...	**Ik wil ...** [ik wil ...]
Do you have ...?	**Hebt u ...?** [hɛpt ju ...?]
Is there a ... here?	**Is hier een ...?** [is hir en ...?]
May I ...?	**Mag ik ...?** [max ik ...?]
..., please (polite request)	**... alstublieft** [... alstu'blift]

I'm looking for ...	**Ik zoek ...** [ik zuk ...]
restroom	**toilet** [twa'lɛt]
ATM	**geldautomaat** [xɛlt·auto'māt]
pharmacy (drugstore)	**apotheek** [apɔ'tēk]
hospital	**ziekenhuis** [zikənhœys]
police station	**politiebureau** [pɔ\'litsi bʉ\'rɔ]
subway	**metro** ['metrɔ]

taxi	**taxi** [taksi]
train station	**station** [sta'tsjɔn]

My name is …	**Ik heet …** [ik hēt …]
What's your name?	**Hoe heet u?** [hu hēt ju?]
Could you please help me?	**Kunt u me helpen alstublieft?** [kʉnt ju mə 'hɛlpən alstʉ'blift?]
I've got a problem.	**Ik heb een probleem.** [ik hɛp en prɔ'blēm]
I don't feel well.	**Ik voel me niet goed.** [ik vul mə nit xut]
Call an ambulance!	**Bel een ambulance!** [bɛl en ambʉ'lansə!]
May I make a call?	**Mag ik opbellen?** [max ik ɔ'bɛlən?]

I'm sorry.	**Sorry.** ['sɔri]
You're welcome.	**Graag gedaan.** [xrāx xə'dān]

I, me	**Ik, mij** [ik, mɛj]
you (inform.)	**jij** [jɛj]
he	**hij** [hɛj]
she	**zij** [zɛj]
they (masc.)	**zij** [zɛj]
they (fem.)	**zij** [zɛj]
we	**wij** [wɛj]
you (pl)	**jullie** ['juli]
you (sg, form.)	**u** [ju]

ENTRANCE	**INGANG** [inxaŋ]
EXIT	**UITGANG** [œʏtxaŋ]
OUT OF ORDER	**BUITEN GEBRUIK** [bœʏtən xə'brœʏk]
CLOSED	**GESLOTEN** [xə'slɔtən]

OPEN	**OPEN** ['ɔpən]
FOR WOMEN	**DAMES** [daməs]
FOR MEN	**HEREN** ['herən]

Questions

Where?	**Waar?** [wār?]
Where to?	**Waarheen?** [wār'hēn?]
Where from?	**Vanwaar?** [van'wār?]
Why?	**Waar?** [wār?]
For what reason?	**Waarom?** [wā'rɔm?]
When?	**Wanneer?** [wa'nēr?]
How long?	**Hoe lang?** [hu laŋ?]
At what time?	**Hoe laat?** [hu lāt?]
How much?	**Hoeveel?** [huvēl?]
Do you have ...?	**Hebt u ...?** [hɛpt ju ...?]
Where is ...?	**Waar is ...?** [wār is ...?]
What time is it?	**Hoe laat is het?** [hu lāt is ət?]
May I make a call?	**Mag ik opbellen?** [max ik ɔ'bɛlən?]
Who's there?	**Wie is daar?** [wi is dār?]
Can I smoke here?	**Mag ik hier roken?** [max ik hir 'rokən?]
May I ...?	**Mag ik ...?** [max ik ...?]

Needs

I'd like ...	**Ik zou graag ...** [ik 'zau xrāx ...]
I don't want ...	**Ik wil niet ...** [ik wil nit ...]
I'm thirsty.	**Ik heb dorst.** [ik hɛp dɔrst]
I want to sleep.	**Ik wil gaan slapen.** [ik wil xān 'slapən]
I want ...	**Ik wil ...** [ik wil ...]
to wash up	**wassen** [wasən]
to brush my teeth	**mijn tanden poetsen** [mɛjn 'tandən 'putsən]
to rest a while	**even rusten** [evən 'rʉstən]
to change my clothes	**me omkleden** [mə 'ɔmkledən]
to go back to the hotel	**teruggaan naar het hotel** [te'rʉxxān nār hɛt hɔ'tɛl]
to buy ...	**... kopen** [... 'kɔpən]
to go to ...	**gaan naar ...** [xān nār ...]
to visit ...	**bezoeken ...** [bə'zukən ...]
to meet with ...	**ontmoeten ...** [ɔnt'mutən ...]
to make a call	**opbellen** [ɔ'bɛlən]
I'm tired.	**Ik ben moe.** [ik bɛn mu]
We are tired.	**We zijn moe.** [we zɛjn mu]
I'm cold.	**Ik heb het koud.** [ik hɛp ət 'kaut]
I'm hot.	**Ik heb het warm.** [ik hɛp ət warm]
I'm OK.	**Ik ben okay.** [ik bɛn ɔ'kɛj]

I need to make a call. **Ik moet opbellen.**
[ik mut ɔ'bɛlən]

I need to go to the restroom. **Ik moet naar het toilet.**
[ik mut nãr ət twa'lɛt]

I have to go. **Ik moet weg.**
[ik mut wɛx]

I have to go now. **Ik moet nu weg.**
[ik mut nʉ wɛx]

Asking for directions

Excuse me, ...	**Pardon, ...** [par'dɔn, ...]
Where is ...?	**Waar is ...?** [wãr is ...?]
Which way is ...?	**Welke richting is ...?** ['wɛlkə 'rixtiŋ is ...?]
Could you help me, please?	**Kunt u me helpen alstublieft?** [kʉnt ju mə 'hɛlpən alstʉ'blift?]

I'm looking for ...	**Ik zoek ...** [ik zuk ...]
I'm looking for the exit.	**Waar is de uitgang?** [wãr is də 'œytxaŋ?]
I'm going to ...	**Ik ga naar ...** [ik xa nãr ...]
Am I going the right way to ...?	**Is dit de weg naar ...?** [is dit də wɛx nãr ...?]

Is it far?	**Is het ver?** [iz ət vɛr?]
Can I get there on foot?	**Kan ik er lopend naar toe?** [kan ik ɛr 'lɔpənt nãr tu?]
Can you show me on the map?	**Kunt u het op de plattegrond aanwijzen?** [kʉnt ju ət ɔp də platə'xrɔnt 'ãnwɛjzən?]
Show me where we are right now.	**Kunt u me aanwijzen waar we nu zijn?** [kʉnt ju mə 'ãnwɛjzən wãr we nʉ zɛjn]

Here	**Hier** [hir]
There	**Daar** [dãr]
This way	**Deze kant uit** [dezə kant 'œyt]

Turn right.	**Rechtsaf.** [rɛxts'af]
Turn left.	**Linksaf.** [linksaf]
first (second, third) turn	**eerste (tweede, derde) bocht** [ẽrstə ('twẽdə, 'dɛrdə) bɔxt]
to the right	**rechtsaf** [rɛxts'af]

to the left **linksaf**
[linksaf]

Go straight ahead. **Ga rechtuit.**
[xa 'rɛxtœɣt]

Signs

WELCOME!	**WELKOM!** ['wɛlkɔm!]
ENTRANCE	**INGANG** [inxaŋ]
EXIT	**UITGANG** [œʏtxaŋ]
PUSH	**DRUK** [drʉk]
PULL	**TREK** [trɛk]
OPEN	**OPEN** ['ɔpən]
CLOSED	**GESLOTEN** [xə'slɔtən]
FOR WOMEN	**DAMES** [daməs]
FOR MEN	**HEREN** ['herən]
GENTLEMEN, GENTS (m)	**HEREN (m)** ['herən]
WOMEN (f)	**DAMES (v)** [daməs]
DISCOUNTS	**KORTINGEN** ['kɔrtiŋən]
SALE	**UITVERKOOP** [œʏt'vɛrkōp]
FREE	**GRATIS** [xratis]
NEW!	**NIEUW!** [niu!]
ATTENTION!	**PAS OP!** [pas ɔp!]
NO VACANCIES	**ALLE KAMERS BEZET** [ale 'kaamərs bə'zɛt]
RESERVED	**GERESERVEERD** [xərezɛr'vērt]
ADMINISTRATION	**ADMINISTRATIE** [administ'ratsi]
STAFF ONLY	**UITSLUITEND PERSONEEL** [œʏtslœʏtənt pɛrsɔ'nēl]

BEWARE OF THE DOG!	**PAS OP VOOR DE HOND!** [pas ɔp vōr də hɔnt!]
NO SMOKING!	**VERBODEN TE ROKEN!** [vər'bɔdən tə 'rɔkən!]
DO NOT TOUCH!	**NIET AANRAKEN!** [nit 'ānrakən!]
DANGEROUS	**GEVAARLIJK** [xe'vārlək]
DANGER	**GEVAAR** [xe'vār]
HIGH VOLTAGE	**HOOGSPANNING** [hōxs'paniŋ]
NO SWIMMING!	**VERBODEN TE ZWEMMEN** [vər'bɔdən tə 'zwemən]

OUT OF ORDER	**BUITEN GEBRUIK** [bœytən xə'brœyk]
FLAMMABLE	**ONTVLAMBAAR** [ɔnt'flambār]
FORBIDDEN	**VERBODEN** [vər'bɔdən]
NO TRESPASSING!	**VERBODEN TOEGANG** [vər'bɔdən 'tuxaŋ]
WET PAINT	**NATTE VERF** [natə vɛrf]

CLOSED FOR RENOVATIONS	**GESLOTEN WEGENS VERBOUWING** [xə'slɔtən 'wexəns vər'bauwiŋ]
WORKS AHEAD	**WERK IN UITVOERING** [wɛrk in œyt'vuriŋ]
DETOUR	**OMWEG** ['ɔmwɛx]

Transportation. General phrases

plane	**vliegtuig** [vlixtœɣx]
train	**trein** [trɛjn]
bus	**bus** [bʉs]
ferry	**veerpont** [vērpɔnt]
taxi	**taxi** [taksi]
car	**auto** [autɔ]
schedule	**dienstregeling** [dinst·'rexəliŋ]
Where can I see the schedule?	**Waar is de dienstregeling?** [wār is də dinst·'rexəliŋ?]
workdays (weekdays)	**werkdagen** [wɛrk'daxən]
weekends	**weekends** [wīkɛnts]
holidays	**vakanties** [va'kantsis]
DEPARTURE	**VERTREK** [vər'trɛk]
ARRIVAL	**AANKOMST** [ānkɔmst]
DELAYED	**VERTRAAGD** [vərt'rāxt]
CANCELLED	**GEANNULEERD** [xəanʉ'lērt]
next (train, etc.)	**volgende** ['vɔlxəndə]
first	**eerste** [ērstə]
last	**laatste** [lātstə]
When is the next ...?	**Hoe laat gaat de volgende ...?** [hu lāt xāt də 'vɔlxəndə ...?]
When is the first ...?	**Hoe laat gaat de eerste ...?** [hu lāt xāt də 'ērstə ...?]

When is the last ...?

Hoe laat gaat de laatste ...?
[hu lāt xāt də 'lātstə ...?]

transfer (change of trains, etc.)

aansluiting
[ānslœүtiŋ]

to make a transfer

overstappen
[ɔvər'stapən]

Do I need to make a transfer?

Moet ik overstappen?
[mut ik ɔvər'stapən?]

Buying tickets

Where can I buy tickets?	**Waar kan ik kaartjes kopen?** [wār kan ik 'kãrtjəs 'kɔpən?]
ticket	**kaartje** [kãrtjə]
to buy a ticket	**een kaartje kopen** [ən 'kãrtjə 'kɔpən]
ticket price	**prijs van een kaartje** [prɛjs van en 'kãrtjə]
Where to?	**Waarheen?** [wār'hēn?]
To what station?	**Naar welk station?** [nãr wɛlk sta'tsjɔn?]
I need ...	**Ik heb ... nodig** [ik hɛp ... 'nɔdəx]
one ticket	**een kaartje** [ən 'kãrtjə]
two tickets	**twee kaartjes** [twē 'kãrtjəs]
three tickets	**drie kaartjes** [dri 'kãrtjəs]
one-way	**enkel** ['ɛnkəl]
round-trip	**retour** [re'tu:r]
first class	**eerste klas** [ērstə klas]
second class	**tweede klas** [twēdə klas]
today	**vandaag** [van'dãx]
tomorrow	**morgen** ['mɔrxən]
the day after tomorrow	**overmorgen** [ɔvər'mɔrxən]
in the morning	**s morgens** [s 'mɔrxəns]
in the afternoon	**s middags** [s 'midaxs]
in the evening	**s avonds** [s 'avɔnts]

aisle seat

zitplaats aan het gangpad
[zitplāts ān ət 'xaŋpat]

window seat

zitplaats bij het raam
[zitplāts bɛj ət rām]

How much?

Hoeveel?
[huvēl?]

Can I pay by credit card?

Kan ik met een creditcard betalen?
[kan ik mɛt en 'kredit·kart bə'talən?]

Bus

bus	**bus** [bʉs]
intercity bus	**intercity bus** [inter'siti bʉs]
bus stop	**bushalte** [bʉs'haltə]
Where's the nearest bus stop?	**Waar is de meest nabij gelegen bushalte?** [wār is də mēst na'bɛj xə'lexən bʉs'haltə?]
number (bus ~, etc.)	**nummer** [nʉmər]
Which bus do I take to get to ...?	**Met welke bus kan ik naar ... gaan?** [mɛt 'wɛlkə bʉs kan ik nār ... xān?]
Does this bus go to ...?	**Gaat deze bus naar ...?** [xāt 'dezə bʉs nār ...?]
How frequent are the buses?	**Hoe dikwijls rijden de bussen?** [hu 'dikwəls 'rɛjdən də 'bʉsən?]
every 15 minutes	**om het kwartier** [ɔm ət kwar'tir]
every half hour	**om het half uur** [ɔm ət half ūr]
every hour	**om het uur** [ɔm ət ūr]
several times a day	**verschillende keren per dag** [vər'sxiləndə 'kerən pər dax]
... times a day	**... keer per dag** [... kēr pər dax]
schedule	**dienstregeling** [dinst·'rexəliŋ]
Where can I see the schedule?	**Waar is de dienstregeling?** [wār is də dinst·'rexəliŋ?]
When is the next bus?	**Hoe laat vertrekt de volgende bus?** [hu lāt vər'trɛkt də 'vɔlxəndə bʉs?]
When is the first bus?	**Hoe laat vertrekt de eerste bus?** [hu lāt vər'trɛkt də 'ērstə bʉs?]
When is the last bus?	**Hoe laat vertrekt de laatste bus?** [hu lāt vər'trɛkt də 'lātstə bʉs?]

stop	**halte** [haltə]
next stop	**volgende halte** [vɔlxəndə 'haltə]
last stop (terminus)	**eindstation** [ɛjnt sta'tsjon]
Stop here, please.	**Hier stoppen alstublieft.** [hir 'stɔpən alstʉ'blift]
Excuse me, this is my stop.	**Pardon, dit is mijn halte.** [par'dɔn, dit is mɛjn 'haltə]

Train

train	**trein** [trɛjn]
suburban train	**pendeltrein** ['pendəl trɛjn]
long-distance train	**langeafstandstrein** [laŋe·'afstants·trɛjn]
train station	**station** [sta'tsjɔn]
Excuse me, where is the exit to the platform?	**Pardon, waar is de toegang tot het perron?** [par'dɔn, wär is də 'tuxaŋ tɔt ət pɛ'rɔn?]
Does this train go to …?	**Gaat deze trein naar …?** [xãt 'dezə trɛjn när …?]
next train	**volgende trein** ['vɔlxəndə trɛjn]
When is the next train?	**Hoe laat gaat de volgende trein?** [hu lãt xãt də 'vɔlxəndə trɛjn?]
Where can I see the schedule?	**Waar is de dienstregeling?** [wär is də dinst·'rexəliŋ?]
From which platform?	**Van welk perron?** [van wɛlk pɛ'rɔn?]
When does the train arrive in …?	**Wanneer komt de trein aan in …?** [wa'nẽr kɔmt də trɛjn ãn in …?]
Please help me.	**Kunt u me helpen alstublieft?** [kʉnt ju mə 'hɛlpən alstʉ'blift?]
I'm looking for my seat.	**Ik zoek mijn zitplaats.** [ik zuk mɛjn 'zitplãts]
We're looking for our seats.	**Wij zoeken onze zitplaatsen.** [wɛj 'zukən 'ɔnzə 'zitplãtsen]
My seat is taken.	**Mijn zitplaats is bezet.** [mɛjn 'zitplãts is bə'zɛt]
Our seats are taken.	**Onze zitplaatsen zijn bezet.** [ɔnzə 'zitplãtsən zɛjn bə'zɛt]
I'm sorry but this is my seat.	**Sorry, maar dit is mijn zitplaats.** [sɔri, mär dit is mɛjn 'zitplãts]
Is this seat taken?	**Is deze zitplaats bezet?** [is 'dezə 'zitplãts bə'zɛt?]
May I sit here?	**Mag ik hier zitten?** [max ik hir 'zitən?]

On the train. Dialogue (No ticket)

Ticket, please.	**Uw kaartje alstublieft.** [ʉw 'kārtjə alstʉ'blift]
I don't have a ticket.	**Ik heb geen kaartje.** [ik hɛp xēn 'kārtjə]
I lost my ticket.	**Ik heb mijn kaartje verloren.** [ik hɛp mɛjn 'kārtjə vər'lɔrən]
I forgot my ticket at home.	**Ik heb mijn kaartje thuis vergeten.** [ik hɛp mɛjn 'kārtjə thœys vər'xetən]
You can buy a ticket from me.	**U kunt een kaartje van mij kopen.** [ju kʉnt ən 'kārtjə van mɛj 'kɔpən]
You will also have to pay a fine.	**U moet ook een boete betalen.** [ju mut ōk ən 'butə bə'talən]
Okay.	**Okay.** [ɔ'kɛj]
Where are you going?	**Waar gaat u naartoe?** [wār xāt ju nārtu?]
I'm going to …	**Ik ga naar …** [ik xa nār …]
How much? I don't understand.	**Hoeveel kost het? Ik versta het niet.** [huvēl kɔst ət? ik vərs'ta ət nit]
Write it down, please.	**Schrijf het neer alstublieft.** [sxrɛjf ət nēr alstʉ'blift]
Okay. Can I pay with a credit card?	**Okay. Kan ik met een creditcard betalen?** [ɔ'kɛj. kan ik mɛt ən 'kredit·kart bə'talən?]
Yes, you can.	**Ja, dat kan.** [ja, dat kan]
Here's your receipt.	**Hier is uw ontvangstbewijs.** [hir is ʉw ɔnt'faŋst·bə'wɛjs]
Sorry about the fine.	**Sorry voor de boete.** [sɔri vōr də 'butə]
That's okay. It was my fault.	**Maakt niet uit. Het is mijn schuld.** [mākt nit œyt hɛt is mɛjn sxʉlt]
Enjoy your trip.	**Prettige reis.** ['prɛtixə rɛjs]

Taxi

taxi	**taxi** [taksi]
taxi driver	**taxi chauffeur** [taksi ʃo'før]
to catch a taxi	**een taxi nemen** [en 'taksi 'nemən]
taxi stand	**taxistandplaats** [taksi·'stantplãts]
Where can I get a taxi?	**Waar kan ik een taxi nemen?** [wãr kan ik en 'taksi 'nemən?]
to call a taxi	**een taxi bellen** [en 'taksi 'bɛlən]
I need a taxi.	**Ik heb een taxi nodig.** [ik hɛp en 'taksi 'nɔdəx]

Right now.	**Nu onmiddellijk.** [nʉ ɔn'midələk]
What is your address (location)?	**Wat is uw adres?** [wat is ʉw ad'rɛs?]
My address is ...	**Mijn adres is ...** [mɛjn ad'rɛs is ...]
Your destination?	**Uw bestemming?** [ʉw bəs'tɛmiŋ?]
Excuse me, ...	**Pardon, ...** [par'dɔn, ...]
Are you available?	**Bent u vrij?** [bɛnt ju vrɛj?]
How much is it to get to ...?	**Hoeveel kost het naar ...?** [huvēl kɔst ət nãr ...?]
Do you know where it is?	**Weet u waar dit is?** [wēt ju wãr dit is?]

Airport, please.	**Luchthaven alstublieft.** [lʉxt'havən alstʉ'blift]
Stop here, please.	**Hier stoppen alstublieft.** [hir 'stɔpən alstʉ'blift]
It's not here.	**Het is niet hier.** [hɛt is nit hir]
This is the wrong address.	**Dit is het verkeerde adres.** [dit is ət vər'kērdə ad'rɛs]
Turn left.	**Linksaf.** [linksaf]
Turn right.	**Rechtsaf.** [rɛxts'af]

How much do I owe you?	**Hoeveel ben ik u schuldig?** [huvēl bɛn ik ju 'sxʉldəx?]
I'd like a receipt, please.	**Kan ik een bon krijgen alstublieft.** [kan ik en bɔn 'krɛjxən alstʉ'blift]
Keep the change.	**Hou het kleingeld maar.** [hau ət 'klɛjnxɛlt mār]

Would you please wait for me?	**Wil u even op mij wachten?** [wil ju 'evən ɔp mɛj 'waxtən?]
five minutes	**vijf minuten** [vɛjf mi'nʉtən]
ten minutes	**tien minuten** [tin mi'nʉtən]
fifteen minutes	**vijftien minuten** [vɛjftin mi'nʉtən]
twenty minutes	**twintig minuten** [twintəx mi'nʉtən]
half an hour	**een half uur** [en half ūr]

Hotel

Hello.	**Hallo.** [halɔ]
My name is …	**Ik heet …** [ik hēt …]
I have a reservation.	**Ik heb gereserveerd.** [ik hɛp xǝrezɛr'vērt]
I need …	**Ik heb … nodig** [ik hɛp … 'nɔdǝx]
a single room	**een enkele kamer** [en 'ɛnkelǝ 'kamǝr]
a double room	**een tweepersoons kamer** [en twē·pɛr'sōns 'kamǝr]
How much is that?	**Hoeveel kost dat?** [huvēl kɔst dat?]
That's a bit expensive.	**Dat is nogal duur.** [dat is 'nɔxal dūr]
Do you have anything else?	**Zijn er geen andere mogelijkheden?** [zɛjn ɛr xēn 'anderǝ 'mɔxǝlǝkhedǝn?]
I'll take it.	**Die neem ik.** [di nēm ik]
I'll pay in cash.	**Ik betaal contant.** [ik bǝ'tāl kɔn'tant]
I've got a problem.	**Ik heb een probleem.** [ik hɛp en prɔ'blēm]
My … is broken.	**Mijn … is stuk.** [mɛjn … is stʉk]
My … is out of order.	**Mijn … doet het niet meer.** [mɛjn … dut ǝt nit mēr]
TV	**TV** [te've]
air conditioner	**airco** ['ɛrkɔ]
tap	**kraan** [krān]
shower	**douche** [duʃ]
sink	**lavabo** [lava'bɔ]
safe	**brandkast** [brantkast]

door lock	**deurslot** ['dørslɔt]
electrical outlet	**stopcontact** [stɔp kɔn'takt]
hairdryer	**haardroger** [hār·drɔxər]

I don't have …	**Ik heb geen …** [ik hɛp xēn …]
water	**water** [watər]
light	**licht** [lixt]
electricity	**stroom** [strōm]

Can you give me …?	**Kunt u mij een … bezorgen?** [kʉnt ju mɛj en … bə'zɔrxən?]
a towel	**een handdoek** [en 'handuk]
a blanket	**een deken** [en 'dekən]
slippers	**pantoffels** [pan'tɔfəls]
a robe	**een badjas** [en badjas]
shampoo	**shampoo** [ʃʌmpō]
soap	**zeep** [zēp]

I'd like to change rooms.	**Ik wil van kamer veranderen.** [ik wil van 'kamər və'randerən]
I can't find my key.	**Ik kan mijn sleutel niet vinden.** [ik kan mɛjn 'sløtel nit 'vindən]
Could you open my room, please?	**Kunt u mijn kamer openen alstublieft?** [kʉnt ju mɛjn 'kamər 'ɔpenən alstʉ'blift?]
Who's there?	**Wie is daar?** [wi is dār?]
Come in!	**Kom binnen!** [kɔm 'binən!]
Just a minute!	**Een ogenblikje!** [en 'ɔxənblikje!]
Not right now, please.	**Niet op dit moment alstublieft.** [nit ɔp dit mɔ'mɛnt alstʉ'blift]

Come to my room, please.	**Kom naar mijn kamer alstublieft.** [kɔm nār mɛjn 'kamər alstʉ'blift]
I'd like to order food service.	**Kan ik room service krijgen.** [kan ik rōm 'sø:rvis 'krɛjxən]
My room number is …	**Mijn kamernummer is …** [mɛjn 'kamər·'nʉmer is …]

I'm leaving ...

Ik vertrek ...
[ik vər'trɛk ...]

We're leaving ...

Wij vertrekken ...
[wɛj vər'trɛkən ...]

right now

nu onmiddellijk
[nʉ ɔn'midələk]

this afternoon

vanmiddag
[van'midax]

tonight

vanavond
[va'navɔnt]

tomorrow

morgen
['mɔrxən]

tomorrow morning

morgenochtend
['mɔrxən 'ɔxtənt]

tomorrow evening

morgenavond
[mɔrxən 'avɔnt]

the day after tomorrow

overmorgen
[ɔvər'mɔrxən]

I'd like to pay.

Ik zou willen afrekenen.
[ik 'zau 'wilən 'afrekənən]

Everything was wonderful.

Alles was uitstekend.
[aləs was œʏts'tekənt]

Where can I get a taxi?

Waar kan ik een taxi nemen?
[wār kan ik en 'taksi 'nemən?]

Would you call a taxi for me, please?

Wil u alstublieft een taxi bestellen?
[wil ju alstʉ'blift en 'taksi bəs'tɛlən?]

Restaurant

Can I look at the menu, please?	**Kan ik het menu zien alstublieft?** [kan ik ət me'nʉ zin alstʉ'blift?]
Table for one.	**Een tafel voor één persoon.** [en 'tafəl võr en pɛr'sōn]
There are two (three, four) of us.	**We zijn met z'n tweeën (drieën, vieren).** [we zɛjn mɛt zən 'twēɛn ('driɛn, 'virən)]

Smoking	**Roken** ['rɔkən]
No smoking	**Niet roken** [nit 'rɔkən]
Excuse me! (addressing a waiter)	**Hallo! Pardon!** [halɔ! par'dɔn!]
menu	**menu** [me'nʉ]
wine list	**wijnkaart** [wɛjnkãrt]
The menu, please.	**Het menu alstublieft.** [hɛt me'nʉ alstʉ'blift]

Are you ready to order?	**Bent u zover om te bestellen?** [bɛnt ju 'zɔvər ɔm tə bəs'tɛlən?]
What will you have?	**Wat wenst u?** [wat wɛnst ju?]
I'll have ...	**Voor mij ...** [võr mɛj ...]

I'm a vegetarian.	**Ik ben vegetariër.** [ik bɛn vexə'tarijər]
meat	**vlees** [vlēs]
fish	**vis** [vis]
vegetables	**groente** ['xruntə]
Do you have vegetarian dishes?	**Hebt u vegetarische gerechten?** [hɛpt ju vexə'tarisə xə'rɛxtən?]
I don't eat pork.	**Ik eet niet varkensvlees.** [ik ēt nit 'varkənsvlēs]
He /she/ doesn't eat meat.	**Hij /zij/ eet geen vlees.** [hɛj /zɛj/ ēt xēn vlēs]

I am allergic to ...

Ik ben allergisch voor ...
[ik bɛn aˈlerxis vōr ...]

Would you please bring me ...

Wil u mij ... brengen
[wil ju mɛj ... bˈrɛŋən]

salt | pepper | sugar

zout | peper | suiker
[zaut | ˈpepər | ˈsœʏkər]

coffee | tea | dessert

koffie | thee | dessert
[kɔfi | tē | dɛˈsɛːr]

water | sparkling | plain

water | met prik | gewoon
[watər | mɛt prik | xəˈwōn]

a spoon | fork | knife

een lepel | vork | mes
[en ˈlepəl | vɔrk | mɛs]

a plate | napkin

een bord | servet
[en bɔrt | sɛrˈvɛt]

Enjoy your meal!

Smakelijk!
[smakələk!]

One more, please.

Nog een alstublieft.
[nɔx en alstʉˈblift]

It was very delicious.

Het was heerlijk.
[hɛt was ˈhērlək]

---

check | change | tip

rekening | wisselgeld | fooi
[rekəniŋ | ˈwisəl·xɛlt | fōj]

Check, please.
(Could I have the check, please?)

De rekening alstublieft.
[də ˈrekəniŋ alstʉˈblift]

Can I pay by credit card?

Kan ik met een creditcard betalen?
[kan ik mɛt en ˈkredit·kart bəˈtalən?]

I'm sorry, there's a mistake here.

Sorry, hier is een fout.
[sɔri, hir iz en ˈfaut]

Shopping

Can I help you?	**Waarmee kan ik u van dienst zijn?** [wãr'mē kan ik ju van dinst zɛjn?]
Do you have ...?	**Hebt u ...?** [hɛpt ju ...?]
I'm looking for ...	**Ik zoek ...** [ik zuk ...]
I need ...	**Ik heb ... nodig** [ik hɛp ... 'nɔdəx]

I'm just looking.	**Ik kijk even.** [ik kɛjk 'evən]
We're just looking.	**Wij kijken even.** [wɛj 'kɛjkən 'evən]
I'll come back later.	**Ik kom wat later terug.** [ik kɔm wat 'latər te'rʉx]
We'll come back later.	**We komen later terug.** [we 'kɔmən 'latər te'rʉx]
discounts | sale	**korting | uitverkoop** [kɔrtiŋ | 'œytverkōp]

Would you please show me ...	**Kunt u mij ... laten zien alstublieft?** [kʉnt ju mɛj ... 'latən zin alstu'blift?]
Would you please give me ...	**Kunt u mij ... geven alstublieft?** [kʉnt ju mɛj ... 'xevən alstu'blift?]
Can I try it on?	**Kan ik dit passen?** [kan ik dit 'pasən?]
Excuse me, where's the fitting room?	**Pardon, waar is de paskamer?** [par'dɔn, wãr is də 'pas·kamər?]

Which color would you like?	**Welke kleur wenst u?** ['wɛlkə 'klør wɛnst ju?]
size | length	**maat | lengte** [mãt | 'leŋtə]
How does it fit?	**Past het?** [past ət?]

How much is it?	**Hoeveel kost het?** [huvēl kɔst ət?]
That's too expensive.	**Dat is te duur.** [dat is tə dūr]
I'll take it.	**Ik neem het.** [ik nēm ət]
Excuse me, where do I pay?	**Pardon, waar moet ik betalen?** [par'dɔn, wãr mut ik bə'talən?]

Will you pay in cash or credit card? | **Betaalt u contant of met een creditcard?**
[bə'tālt ju kɔn'tant ɔf mɛt en 'kredit·kart?]

In cash | with credit card | **contant | met een creditcard**
[kɔn'tant | mɛt en 'kredit·kart]

Do you want the receipt? | **Wil u een kwitantie?**
[wil ju en kwi'tantsi?]

Yes, please. | **Ja graag.**
[ja xrāx]

No, it's OK. | **Nee, hoeft niet.**
[nē, huft nit]

Thank you. Have a nice day! | **Bedankt. Een fijne dag verder!**
[bə'dankt. en 'fɛjnə dax 'vɛrdər!]

In town

Excuse me, please.	**Pardon, ...** [par'dɔn, ...]
I'm looking for ...	**Ik ben op zoek naar ...** [ik bɛn ɔp zuk nār ...]

the subway	**de metro** [də 'metrɔ]
my hotel	**mijn hotel** [mɛjn hɔ'tɛl]
the movie theater	**de bioscoop** [də biɔ'skōp]
a taxi stand	**een taxistandplaats** [en 'taksi·'stantplāts]

an ATM	**een geldautomaat** [en xɛlt·autɔ'māt]
a foreign exchange office	**een wisselagent** [en 'wisəl·a'xɛnt]
an internet café	**een internet café** [en 'intərnɛt ka'fe]
... street	**... straat** [... strāt]
this place	**dit adres** [dit ad'rɛs]

Do you know where ... is?	**Weet u waar ... is?** [wēt ju wār ... is?]
Which street is this?	**Welke straat is dit?** [wɛlkə strāt is dit?]

Show me where we are right now.	**Kunt u me aanwijzen waar we nu zijn?** [kʉnt ju mə 'ānwɛjzən wār wə nʉ zɛjn]
Can I get there on foot?	**Kan ik er lopend naar toe?** [kan ik ɛr 'lɔpənt nār tu?]
Do you have a map of the city?	**Hebt u een plattegrond van de stad?** [hɛpt ju en platə'xrɔnt van də stat?]

How much is a ticket to get in?	**Hoeveel kost de toegang?** [huvēl kɔst də 'tuxaŋ?]
Can I take pictures here?	**Kan ik hier foto's maken?** [kan ik hir 'fotɔs 'makən?]
Are you open?	**Bent u open?** [bɛnt ju 'ɔpən?]

When do you open?

Hoe laat gaat u open?
[hu lāt xāt ju 'ɔpən?]

When do you close?

Hoe laat sluit u?
[hu lāt slœʏt ju?]

Money

money	**geld** [xɛlt]
cash	**contant** [kɔn'tant]
paper money	**bankbiljetten** [bank·bi'ljetən]
loose change	**kleingeld** [klɛjn·xɛlt]
check | change | tip	**rekening | wisselgeld | fooi** [rekəniŋ | 'wisəl·xɛlt | fõj]
credit card	**creditcard** [kredit·kart]
wallet	**portemonnee** [pɔrtəmɔ'nē]
to buy	**kopen** ['kɔpən]
to pay	**betalen** [bə'talən]
fine	**boete** ['butə]
free	**gratis** [xratis]
Where can I buy ...?	**Waar kan ik ... kopen?** [wār kan ik ... 'kɔpən?]
Is the bank open now?	**Is de bank nu open?** [is də bank nʉ 'ɔpən?]
When does it open?	**Hoe laat gaat hij open?** [hu lāt xāt hɛj 'ɔpən?]
When does it close?	**Hoe laat sluit hij?** [hu lāt slœyt hɛj?]
How much?	**Hoeveel?** [huvēl?]
How much is this?	**Hoeveel kost dit?** [huvēl kɔst dit?]
That's too expensive.	**Dat is te duur.** [dat is tə dūr]
Excuse me, where do I pay?	**Pardon, waar moet ik betalen?** [par'dɔn, wār mut ik bə'talən?]
Check, please.	**De rekening alstublieft.** [də 'rekəniŋ alstʉ'blift]

Can I pay by credit card? **Kan ik met een creditcard betalen?**
[kan ik mɛt en 'kredit·kart bə'talən?]

Is there an ATM here? **Is hier een geldautomaat?**
[is hir en xɛlt·autɔ'māt?]

I'm looking for an ATM. **Ik zoek een geldautomaat.**
[ik zuk en xɛlt·autɔ'māt]

I'm looking for a foreign exchange office. **Ik zoek een wisselagent.**
[ik zuk en 'wisəl a'xɛnt]

I'd like to change … **Ik zou … willen wisselen.**
[ik 'zau … 'wilən 'wisələn]

What is the exchange rate? **Wat is de wisselkoers?**
[wat is də 'wisəl·kurs?]

Do you need my passport? **Hebt u mijn paspoort nodig?**
[hɛpt ju mɛjn 'paspõrt 'nɔdəx?]

Time

What time is it?	**Hoe laat is het?** [hu lāt is ət?]
When?	**Wanneer?** [wa'nēr?]
At what time?	**Hoe laat?** [hu lāt?]
now | later | after …	**nu | later | na …** [nʉ | 'latər | na …]
one o'clock	**een uur** [en ūr]
one fifteen	**kwart over een** [kwart 'ɔvər en]
one thirty	**half twee** [half twē]
one forty-five	**kwart voor twee** [kwart vōr twē]
one | two | three	**een | twee | drie** [en | twē | dri]
four | five | six	**vier | vijf | zes** [vir | vɛjf | zɛs]
seven | eight | nine	**zeven | acht | negen** [zevən | axt | 'nexən]
ten | eleven | twelve	**tien | elf | twaalf** [tin | ɛlf | twālf]
in …	**binnen …** ['binən …]
five minutes	**vijf minuten** [vɛjf mi'nʉtən]
ten minutes	**tien minuten** [tin mi'nʉtən]
fifteen minutes	**vijftien minuten** [vɛjftin mi'nʉtən]
twenty minutes	**twintig minuten** [twintəx mi'nʉtən]
half an hour	**een half uur** [en half ūr]
an hour	**een uur** [en ūr]

in the morning	**s ochtends** [s 'ɔxtənts]
early in the morning	**s ochtends vroeg** [s 'ɔxtənts vrux]
this morning	**vanmorgen** [van'mɔrxən]
tomorrow morning	**morgenochtend** ['mɔrxən 'ɔxtənt]

in the middle of the day	**in het midden van de dag** [in ət 'midən van də dax]
in the afternoon	**s middags** [s 'midaxs]
in the evening	**s avonds** [s 'avɔnts]
tonight	**vanavond** [va'navɔnt]

at night	**s avonds** [s 'avɔnts]
yesterday	**gisteren** ['xistərən]
today	**vandaag** [van'dāx]
tomorrow	**morgen** ['mɔrxən]
the day after tomorrow	**overmorgen** [ɔvər'mɔrxən]

What day is it today?	**Wat is het vandaag?** [wat is ət van'dāx?]
It's …	**Het is …** [hɛt is …]
Monday	**maandag** [māndax]
Tuesday	**dinsdag** [dinzdax]
Wednesday	**woensdag** [wunzdax]

Thursday	**donderdag** [dɔndərdax]
Friday	**vrijdag** [vrɛjdax]
Saturday	**zaterdag** [zatərdax]
Sunday	**zondag** [zɔndax]

Greetings. Introductions

Hello.
Hallo.
[halɔ]

Pleased to meet you.
Aangenaam.
[ānxənām]

Me too.
Insgelijks.
['insxeləks]

I'd like you to meet …
Mag ik u voorstellen aan …
[max ik ju 'vōrstɛlən ān …]

Nice to meet you.
Aangenaam.
[ānxənām]

How are you?
Hoe gaat het met u?
[hu xāt ət mɛt ju?]

My name is …
Ik heet …
[ik hēt …]

His name is …
Dit is …
[dit is …]

Her name is …
Dit is …
[dit is …]

What's your name?
Hoe heet u?
[hu hēt ju?]

What's his name?
Hoe heet hij?
[hu hēt hɛj?]

What's her name?
Hoe heet zij?
[hu hēt zɛj?]

What's your last name?
Wat is uw achternaam?
[wat is ʉw 'axtər·nām?]

You can call me …
Noem mij maar …
[num mɛj mār …]

Where are you from?
Vanwaar komt u?
[van'wār komt ju?]

I'm from …
Ik kom van …
[ik kom van …]

What do you do for a living?
Wat is uw beroep?
[wat is ʉw bə'rup?]

Who is this?
Wie is dit?
[wi is dit?]

Who is he?
Wie is hij?
[wi is hɛj?]

Who is she?
Wie is zij?
[wi is zɛj?]

Who are they?
Wie zijn zij?
[wi zɛjn zɛj?]

This is ...	**Dit is ...** [dit is ...]
my friend (masc.)	**mijn vriend** [mɛjn vrint]
my friend (fem.)	**mijn vriendin** [mɛjn vrin'din]
my husband	**mijn man** [mɛjn man]
my wife	**mijn vrouw** [mɛjn 'vrau]
my father	**mijn vader** [mɛjn 'vadər]
my mother	**mijn moeder** [mɛjn 'mudər]
my brother	**mijn broer** [mɛjn brur]
my sister	**mijn zuster** [mɛjn 'zʉstər]
my son	**mijn zoon** [mɛjn zõn]
my daughter	**mijn dochter** [mɛjn 'dɔxtər]
This is our son.	**Dit is onze zoon.** [dit is 'ɔnzə zõn]
This is our daughter.	**Dit is onze dochter.** [dit is 'ɔnzə 'dɔxtər]
These are my children.	**Dit zijn mijn kinderen.** [dit zɛjn 'mɛjn 'kindərən]
These are our children.	**Dit zijn onze kinderen.** [dit zɛjn 'ɔnzə 'kindərən]

Farewells

Good bye!	**Tot ziens!** [tɔt zins!]
Bye! (inform.)	**Doei!** [dui!]
See you tomorrow.	**Tot morgen.** [tɔt 'mɔrxən]
See you soon.	**Tot binnenkort.** [tɔt binə'kɔrt]
See you at seven.	**Tot om zeven uur.** [tɔt ɔm 'zevən ūr]
Have fun!	**Veel plezier!** [vēl plə'zīr!]
Talk to you later.	**Tot straks.** [tɔt straks]
Have a nice weekend.	**Prettig weekend.** [prɛtəx 'wīkɛnt]
Good night.	**Goede nacht.** [xudə naxt]
It's time for me to go.	**ik moet opstappen.** [ik mut 'ɔpstapən]
I have to go.	**Ik moet weg.** [ik mut wɛx]
I will be right back.	**ik ben zo terug.** [ik bɛn zɔ te'rʉx]
It's late.	**Het is al laat.** [hɛt is al lāt]
I have to get up early.	**Ik moet vroeg op.** [ik mut vrux ɔp]
I'm leaving tomorrow.	**Ik vertrek morgen.** [ik vər'trɛk 'mɔrxən]
We're leaving tomorrow.	**Wij vertrekken morgen.** [wɛj vər'trɛkən 'mɔrxən]
Have a nice trip!	**Prettige reis!** ['prɛtixə rɛjs!]
It was nice meeting you.	**Het was fijn u te leren kennen.** [hɛt was fɛjn ju tə 'lerən 'kɛnən]
It was nice talking to you.	**Het was een prettig gesprek.** [hɛt was ən 'prɛtəx xe'sprɛk]
Thanks for everything.	**Dank u wel voor alles.** [dank ju wɛl vōr 'aləs]

I had a very good time.

ik heb ervan genoten.
[ik hɛp ɛr'van xe'nɔtən]

We had a very good time.

Wij hebben ervan genoten.
[wɛj 'hɛbən ɛr'van xə'nɔtən]

It was really great.

Het was bijzonder leuk.
[hɛt was bi'zɔndər 'løk]

I'm going to miss you.

Ik ga je missen.
[ik xa je 'misən]

We're going to miss you.

Wij gaan je missen.
[wɛj xān je 'misən]

Good luck!

Veel succes!
[vēl sʉk'sɛs!]

Say hi to …

De groeten aan …
[də 'xrutən ān …]

Foreign language

I don't understand.	**Ik versta het niet.** [ik vər'sta ət nit]
Write it down, please.	**Schrijf het neer alstublieft.** [sxrɛjf ət nẽr alstʉ'blift]
Do you speak ...?	**Spreekt u ...?** [sprẽkt ju ...?]
I speak a little bit of ...	**Ik spreek een beetje ...** [ik sprẽk en 'bẽtjə ...]
English	**Engels** ['ɛŋəls]
Turkish	**Turks** [tʉrks]
Arabic	**Arabisch** [a'rabis]
French	**Frans** [frans]
German	**Duits** [dœyts]
Italian	**Italiaans** [itali'ãns]
Spanish	**Spaans** [spãns]
Portuguese	**Portugees** [portʉ'xẽs]
Chinese	**Chinees** [ʃi'nẽs]
Japanese	**Japans** [ja'pans]
Can you repeat that, please.	**Kunt u dat herhalen alstublieft.** [kʉnt ju dat hɛr'halən alstʉ'blift]
I understand.	**Ik versta het.** [ik vər'sta ət]
I don't understand.	**Ik versta het niet.** [ik vər'sta ət nit]
Please speak more slowly.	**Spreek wat langzamer alstublieft.** [sprẽk wat 'laŋzamər alstʉ'blift]
Is that correct? (Am I saying it right?)	**Is dat juist?** [is dat jœyst?]
What is this? (What does this mean?)	**Wat is dit?** [wat is dit?]

Apologies

Excuse me, please.	**Excuseer me alstublieft.** [ɛkskʉ'zēr mə alstʉ'blift]
I'm sorry.	**Sorry.** ['sɔri]
I'm really sorry.	**Het spijt me.** [hɛt spɛjt mə]
Sorry, it's my fault.	**Sorry, het is mijn schuld.** [sɔri, hɛt is mɛjn sxʉlt]
My mistake.	**Mijn schuld.** [mɛjn sxʉlt]
May I ...?	**Mag ik ...?** [max ik ...?]
Do you mind if I ...?	**Is het goed dat ...?** [iz ət xut dat ...?]
It's OK.	**Het is okay.** [hɛt is ɔ'kɛj]
It's all right.	**Maakt niet uit.** [mākt nit œyt]
Don't worry about it.	**Maak je geen zorgen.** [māk jə xēn 'zɔrxən]

Agreement

Yes. | **Ja.**
[ja]

Yes, sure. | **Ja zeker.**
[ja 'zekər]

OK (Good!) | **Goed!**
[xut!]

Very well. | **Uitstekend.**
[œyt'stekənt]

Certainly! | **Zeker weten!**
['zekər 'wetən!]

I agree. | **Ik ga akkoord.**
[ik xa a'kõrt]

That's correct. | **Precies.**
[prə'sis]

That's right. | **Juist.**
[jœyst]

You're right. | **Je hebt gelijk.**
[je hɛpt xə'lɛjk]

I don't mind. | **Ik doe het graag.**
[ik du ət xrãx]

Absolutely right. | **Dat is juist.**
[dat is jœyst]

It's possible. | **Dat is mogelijk.**
[dat is 'mɔxələk]

That's a good idea. | **Dat is een goed idee.**
[dat is ən xut i'dē]

I can't say no. | **Ik kan niet nee zeggen.**
[ik kan nit nē 'zɛxən]

I'd be happy to. | **Met genoegen.**
[mɛt xə'nuxən]

With pleasure. | **Graag.**
[xrãx]

Refusal. Expressing doubt

No.	**Nee.** [nē]
Certainly not.	**Beslist niet.** [bəs'list nit]
I don't agree.	**Daar ben ik het niet mee eens.** [dār bɛn ik ət nit mē ēns]
I don't think so.	**Dat geloof ik niet.** [dat xe'lōf ik nit]
It's not true.	**Dat is niet waar.** [dat is nit wār]
You are wrong.	**U maakt een fout.** [ju mākt en 'faut]
I think you are wrong.	**Ik denk dat u een fout maakt.** [ik dɛnk dat ju en 'faut mākt]
I'm not sure.	**Ik weet het niet zeker.** [ik wēt ət nit 'zekər]
It's impossible.	**Het is onmogelijk.** [hɛt is ɔn'mɔxələk]
Nothing of the kind (sort)!	**Beslist niet!** [bəs'list nit!]
The exact opposite.	**Precies het tegenovergestelde!** [prə'sis hɛt 'texən·'ɔvərxəstɛldə!]
I'm against it.	**Ik ben er tegen.** [ik bɛn ɛr 'texən]
I don't care.	**Ik geef er niet om.** [ik xēf ɛr nit ɔm]
I have no idea.	**Ik heb geen idee.** [ik hɛp xēn i'dē]
I doubt it.	**Dat betwijfel ik.** [dat bet'wɛjfəl ik]
Sorry, I can't.	**Sorry, ik kan niet.** [sɔri, ik kan nit]
Sorry, I don't want to.	**Sorry, ik wil niet.** ['sɔri, ik wil nit]
Thank you, but I don't need this.	**Dank u, maar ik heb dit niet nodig.** [dank ju, mār ik hɛp dit nit 'nɔdəx]
It's getting late.	**Het wordt laat.** [hɛt wɔrt lāt]

I have to get up early.

Ik moet vroeg op.
[ik mut vrux ɔp]

I don't feel well.

Ik voel me niet lekker.
[ik vul mə nit 'lɛkər]

Expressing gratitude

Thank you.	**Bedankt.** [bə'dankt]
Thank you very much.	**Heel erg bedankt.** [hēl ɛrx bə'dankt]
I really appreciate it.	**Ik stel dit zeer op prijs.** [ik stel dit zēr ɔp prɛjs]
I'm really grateful to you.	**Ik ben u erg dankbaar.** [ik bɛn ju ɛrx 'dankbār]
We are really grateful to you.	**Wij zijn u erg dankbaar.** [wɛj zɛjn ju ɛrx 'dankbār]
Thank you for your time.	**Bedankt voor uw tijd.** [bə'dankt vōr ʉw tɛjt]
Thanks for everything.	**Dank u wel voor alles.** [dank ju wɛl vōr 'aləs]
Thank you for ...	**Bedankt voor ...** [bə'dankt vōr ...]
your help	**uw hulp** [ʉw hʉlp]
a nice time	**een leuke dag** [en 'løkə dax]
a wonderful meal	**een heerlijke maaltijd** [en 'hērlɛkə 'māltɛjt]
a pleasant evening	**een prettige avond** [en 'prɛtixə 'avɔnt]
a wonderful day	**een prettige dag** [en 'prɛtixə dax]
an amazing journey	**een fantastische reis** [en fan'tastise rɛjs]
Don't mention it.	**Graag gedaan.** [xrãx xə'dãn]
You are welcome.	**Graag gedaan.** [xrãx xə'dãn]
Any time.	**Graag gedaan.** [xrãx xə'dãn]
My pleasure.	**Tot uw dienst.** [tɔt ʉw dinst]
Forget it.	**Graag gedaan.** [xrãx xə'dãn]
Don't worry about it.	**Maak je geen zorgen.** [mãk je xẽn 'zɔrxən]

Congratulations. Best wishes

Congratulations!	**Gefeliciteerd!** [xəfelisi'tẽrt!]
Happy birthday!	**Gefeliciteerd met je verjaardag!** [xəfelisi'tẽrt mɛt je və'rjãrdax!]
Merry Christmas!	**Prettig Kerstfeest!** [prɛtəx 'kɛrstfẽst!]
Happy New Year!	**Gelukkig Nieuwjaar!** [xə'lʉkəx 'niu'jãr!]
Happy Easter!	**Vrolijk Paasfeest!** [vrɔlək 'pãsfẽst!]
Happy Hanukkah!	**Gelukkig Chanoeka!** [xə'lʉkəx 'xanuka!]
I'd like to propose a toast.	**Ik wil een heildronk uitbrengen.** [ik wil en 'hɛjldrɔnk 'œytbreɲen]
Cheers!	**Proost!** [prõst!]
Let's drink to …!	**Laten we drinken op …!** [latən we 'drinkən ɔp … !]
To our success!	**Op ons succes!** [ɔp ɔns sʉk'sɛs!]
To your success!	**Op uw succes!** [ɔp ʉw sʉk'sɛs!]
Good luck!	**Veel succes!** [vẽl sʉk'sɛs!]
Have a nice day!	**Een prettige dag!** [en 'prɛtixə dax!]
Have a good holiday!	**Een prettige vakantie!** [en 'prɛtixə va'kantsi!]
Have a safe journey!	**Een veilige reis!** [en 'vɛjlixə rɛjs!]
I hope you get better soon!	**Ik hoop dat u gauw weer beter bent!** [ik hõp dat ju 'xau wẽr 'betər bɛnt!]

Socializing

Why are you sad?

Waarom zie je er zo verdrietig uit?
[wā'rɔm zi je ɛr zɔ vər'dritəx œʏt?]

Smile! Cheer up!

Lach eens! Wees vrolijk!
[lax ēns! wēs 'vrɔlək!]

Are you free tonight?

Ben je vrij vanavond?
[bɛn je vrɛj va'navɔnt?]

May I offer you a drink?

Mag ik je een drankje aanbieden?
[max ik je en 'drankje 'ānbidən?]

Would you like to dance?

Zullen we eens dansen?
[zʉlən we ēns 'dansən?]

Let's go to the movies.

Laten we naar de bioscoop gaan.
[latən we nār də biɔ'skōp xān]

May I invite you to ...?

Mag ik je uitnodigen naar ...?
[max ik je 'œʏtnɔdixən nār ...?]

a restaurant

een restaurant
[en rɛstɔ'ran]

the movies

de bioscoop
[də biɔ'skōp]

the theater

het theater
[hɛt te'ater]

go for a walk

een wandeling
[en 'wandəliŋ]

At what time?

Hoe laat?
[hu lāt?]

tonight

vanavond
[va'navɔnt]

at six

om zes uur
[ɔm zɛs ūr]

at seven

om zeven uur
[ɔm 'zevən ūr]

at eight

om acht uur
[ɔm axt ūr]

at nine

om negen uur
[ɔm 'nexən ūr]

Do you like it here?

Vind u het hier leuk?
[vint ju ət hir 'løk?]

Are you here with someone?

Bent u hier met iemand?
[bɛnt ju hir mɛt i'mant?]

I'm with my friend.

Ik ben met mijn vriend.
[ik bɛn mɛt mɛjn vrint]

I'm with my friends.

Ik ben met mijn vrienden.
[ik bɛn mɛt mɛjn 'vrindən]

No, I'm alone.

Nee, ik ben alleen.
[ik bɛn a'lēn]

Do you have a boyfriend?

Heb jij een vriendje?
[hɛp jɛj en 'vrindje?]

I have a boyfriend.

Ik heb een vriendje.
[ik hɛp en 'vrindje]

Do you have a girlfriend?

Heb jij een vriendin?
[hɛp jɛj en vrin'din?]

I have a girlfriend.

Ik heb een vriendin.
[ik hɛp en vrin'din]

Can I see you again?

Kan ik je weer eens zien?
[kan ik je wēr ēns zin?]

Can I call you?

Mag ik je opbellen?
[max ik je ɔ'bɛlən?]

Call me. (Give me a call.)

Bel me op.
[bɛl mə ɔp]

What's your number?

Wat is je nummer?
[wat is je 'nʉmər?]

I miss you.

Ik mis je.
[ik mis je]

You have a beautiful name.

U hebt een mooie naam.
[ju hɛpt en mōje nām]

I love you.

Ik hou van jou.
[ik 'hau van 'jau]

Will you marry me?

Wil je met me trouwen?
[wil je mɛt mə 'trauwən?]

You're kidding!

Dat meen je niet!
[dat mēn je nit!]

I'm just kidding.

Grapje.
[xrapje]

Are you serious?

Meen je dat?
[mēn je dat?]

I'm serious.

Ik meen het.
[ik mēn ət]

Really?!

Heus waar?!
[høs wār?!]

It's unbelievable!

Dat is ongelooflijk!
[dat is ɔnxə'lōflək!]

I don't believe you.

Ik geloof je niet.
[ik xə'lōf je nit]

I can't.

Ik kan niet.
[ik kan nit]

I don't know.

Ik weet het niet.
[ik wēt ət nit]

I don't understand you.

Ik versta u niet.
[ik vər'sta ju nit]

Please go away.

Ga alstublieft weg.
[xa alstʉ'blift wɛx]

Leave me alone!

Laat me gerust!
[lāt mə xə'rʉst!]

I can't stand him.

Ik kan hem niet uitstaan.
[ik kan hɛm nit 'œʏtstān]

You are disgusting!

U bent een smeerlap!
[ju bɛnt en 'smērlap!]

I'll call the police!

Ik ga de politie bellen!
[ik xa də pɔ'litsi 'bɛlən!]

Sharing impressions. Emotions

I like it.	**Dat vind ik fijn.** [dat vint ik fɛjn]
Very nice.	**Heel mooi.** [hēl mōj]
That's great!	**Wat leuk!** [wat 'løk!]
It's not bad.	**Dat is niet slecht.** [dat is nit slɛxt]

I don't like it.	**Daar houd ik niet van.** [dār 'haut ik nit van]
It's not good.	**Dat is niet goed.** [dat is nit xut]
It's bad.	**Het is slecht.** [hɛt is slɛxt]
It's very bad.	**Het is heel slecht.** [hɛt is hēl slɛxt]
It's disgusting.	**Het is smerig.** [hɛt is 'smerəx]

I'm happy.	**Ik ben blij.** [ik bɛn blɛj]
I'm content.	**Ik ben tevreden.** [ik bɛn təv'redən]
I'm in love.	**ik ben verliefd.** [ik bɛn vər'lift]
I'm calm.	**Ik voel me rustig.** [ik vul mə 'rʉstəx]
I'm bored.	**Ik verveel me.** [ik vər'vēl mə]

I'm tired.	**Ik ben moe.** [ik bɛn mu]
I'm sad.	**Ik ben verdrietig.** [ik bɛn vər'dritəx]
I'm frightened.	**Ik ben bang.** [ik bɛn baŋ]

I'm angry.	**Ik ben kwaad.** [ik bɛn kwāt]
I'm worried.	**Ik ben bezorgd.** [ik bɛn bə'zɔrxt]
I'm nervous.	**Ik ben zenuwachtig.** [ik bɛn 'zenʉwaxtəx]

I'm jealous. (envious)

Ik ben jaloers.
[ik bɛn jaˈlurs]

I'm surprised.

Het verwondert me.
[hɛt vərˈwɔndərt mə]

I'm perplexed.

Ik sta paf.
[ik sta paf]

Problems. Accidents

I've got a problem.	**Ik heb een probleem.** [ik hɛp en prɔ'blēm]
We've got a problem.	**Wij hebben een probleem.** [wɛj 'hɛbən en prɔ'blēm]
I'm lost.	**Ik ben de weg kwijt.** [ik bɛn də wɛx kwɛjt]
I missed the last bus (train).	**Ik heb de laatste bus (trein) gemist.** [ik hɛp də 'lātstə bus (trɛjn) xə'mist]
I don't have any money left.	**Ik heb geen geld meer.** [ik hɛp xēn xɛlt mēr]

I've lost my ...	**Ik heb mijn ... verloren** [ik hɛp mɛjn ... vər'lɔrən]
Someone stole my ...	**Iemand heeft mijn ... gestolen** [imant hēft mɛjn ... xəs'tɔlən]
passport	**paspoort** [paspōrt]
wallet	**portemonnee** [pɔrtəmɔ'nē]
papers	**papieren** [pa'pirən]
ticket	**kaartje** [kārtjə]

money	**geld** [xɛlt]
handbag	**tas** [tas]
camera	**camera** [kaməra]
laptop	**laptop** ['lɛptɔp]
tablet computer	**tablet** [tab'lɛt]
mobile phone	**mobieltje** [mɔ'biltjə]

Help me!	**Help!** [hɛlp!]
What's happened?	**Wat is er aan de hand?** [wat is ɛr ān də hant?]
fire	**brand** [brant]

shooting	**er wordt geschoten** [ɛr wɔrt xəs'xɔtən]
murder	**moord** [mõrt]
explosion	**ontploffing** [ɔntp'lɔfiŋ]
fight	**gevecht** [xə'vɛxt]

Call the police!	**Bel de politie!** [bɛl də pɔ'litsi!]
Please hurry up!	**Opschieten alstublieft!** [ɔpsxitən alstʉ'blift!]
I'm looking for the police station.	**Ik zoek het politiebureau.** [ik zuk ət pɔ'litsi bʉ'rɔ]
I need to make a call.	**Ik moet opbellen.** [ik mut ɔ'bɛlən]
May I use your phone?	**Mag ik uw telefoon gebruiken?** [max ik ʉw telə'fõn xə'brœʏkən?]

I've been …	**Ik ben …** [ik bɛn …]
mugged	**overvallen** [ɔvər'valən]
robbed	**bestolen** [bəs'tɔlən]
raped	**verkracht** [vərk'raxt]
attacked (beaten up)	**aangevallen** [ānxəvalən]

Are you all right?	**Gaat het?** [xāt ət?]
Did you see who it was?	**Hebt u gezien wie het was?** [hɛpt ju xə'zin wi ət was?]
Would you be able to recognize the person?	**Zou u de persoon kunnen herkennen?** [zau ju də pɛr'sõn 'kʉnən hɛr'kɛnən?]
Are you sure?	**Bent u daar zeker van?** [bɛnt ju dār 'zekər van?]

Please calm down.	**Rustig aan alstublieft.** [rʉstəx ān alstʉ'blift]
Take it easy!	**Kalm aan!** [kalm ān!]
Don't worry!	**Maak je geen zorgen!** [māk je xēn 'zɔrxən!]
Everything will be fine.	**Alles komt in orde.** [aləs kɔmt in 'ɔrdə]
Everything's all right.	**Alles is in orde.** [aləs iz in 'ɔrdə]
Come here, please.	**Kom hier alstublieft.** [kɔm hir alstʉ'blift]

I have some questions for you.

Ik heb een paar vragen voor u.
[ik hɛp en pãr 'vraxən võr ju]

Wait a moment, please.

Een ogenblikje alstublieft.
[en 'ɔxənblikje alstʉ'blift]

Do you have any I.D.?

Hebt u een ID-kaart?
[hɛpt ju en aj'di-kãrt?]

Thanks. You can leave now.

Dank u. U mag nu vertrekken.
[dank ju. ju max nʉ vər'trɛkən]

Hands behind your head!

Handen achter uw hoofd!
[handən 'axtər ʉw hõft!]

You're under arrest!

U bent onder arrest!
[ju bɛnt 'ɔndər a'rɛst!]

Health problems

Please help me.	**Kunt u mij helpen alstublieft?** [kʉnt ju mɛj 'hɛlpən alstʉ'blift]
I don't feel well.	**Ik voel me niet goed.** [ik vul mə nit xut]
My husband doesn't feel well.	**Mijn man voelt zich niet goed.** [mɛjn man vult zix nit xut]
My son ...	**Mijn zoon ...** [mɛjn zõn ...]
My father ...	**Mijn vader ...** [mɛjn 'vadər ...]
My wife doesn't feel well.	**Mijn vrouw voelt zich niet goed.** [mɛjn 'vrau vult zix nit xut]
My daughter ...	**Mijn dochter ...** [mɛjn 'dɔxtər ...]
My mother ...	**Mijn moeder ...** [mɛjn 'mudər ...]
I've got a ...	**Ik heb ...** [ik hɛp ...]
headache	**hoofdpijn** [hõftpɛjn]
sore throat	**keelpijn** [kẽlpɛjn]
stomach ache	**maagpijn** [mãxpɛjn]
toothache	**tandpijn** [tantpɛjn]
I feel dizzy.	**Ik voel me duizelig.** [ik vul mə 'dœyzələx]
He has a fever.	**Hij heeft koorts.** [hɛj hẽft kõrts]
She has a fever.	**Zij heeft koorts.** [zɛj hẽft kõrts]
I can't breathe.	**Ik heb moeite met ademen.** [ik hɛp 'mujtə mɛt 'adəmən]
I'm short of breath.	**Ik ben kortademig.** [ik bɛn kɔ'rtadəməx]
I am asthmatic.	**Ik ben astmatisch.** [ik bɛn astm'atis]
I am diabetic.	**Ik ben diabeet.** [ik bɛn 'diabẽt]

I can't sleep.
Ik kan niet slapen.
[ik kan nit 'slapǝn]

food poisoning
voedselvergiftiging
[vutsǝl·vǝr'xiftǝxiŋ]

It hurts here.
Het doet hier pijn.
[hɛt dut hir pɛjn]

Help me!
Help!
[hɛlp!]

I am here!
Ik ben hier!
[ik bɛn hir!]

We are here!
Wij zijn hier!
[wɛj zɛjn hir!]

Get me out of here!
Kom mij halen!
[kɔm mɛj 'halǝn!]

I need a doctor.
Ik heb een dokter nodig.
[ik hɛp en 'dɔktǝr 'nɔdǝx]

I can't move.
Ik kan me niet bewegen.
[ik kan mǝ nit bǝ'wexǝn]

I can't move my legs.
Ik kan mijn benen niet bewegen.
[ik kan mɛjn 'benǝn nit bǝ'wexǝn]

I have a wound.
Ik heb een wond.
[ik hɛp en wɔnt]

Is it serious?
Is het erg?
[iz ǝt ɛrx?]

My documents are in my pocket.
Mijn documenten zijn in mijn zak.
[mɛjn dɔkʉ'mɛntǝn zɛjn in mɛjn zak]

Calm down!
Rustig maar!
[rʉstǝx mãr!]

May I use your phone?
Mag ik uw telefoon gebruiken?
[max ik ʉw telǝ'fõn xe'brœykǝn?]

Call an ambulance!
Bel een ambulance!
[bɛl en ambʉ'lansǝ!]

It's urgent!
Het is dringend!
[hɛt is 'driŋǝnt!]

It's an emergency!
Het is een noodgeval!
[hɛt is en 'nõtxǝval!]

Please hurry up!
Opschieten alstublieft!
[ɔpsxitǝn alstʉ'blift!]

Would you please call a doctor?
Kunt u alstublieft een dokter bellen?
[kʉnt ju alstʉ'blift en 'dɔktǝr 'bɛlǝn?]

Where is the hospital?
Waar is het ziekenhuis?
[wãr iz ǝt 'zikǝnhœys?]

How are you feeling?
Hoe voelt u zich?
[hu vult ju zix?]

Are you all right?
Hoe gaat het?
[hu xãt ǝt?]

What's happened?
Wat is er gebeurd?
[wat is ɛr xǝ'børt?]

I feel better now.

Ik voel me nu wat beter.
[ik vul mə nʉ wat 'betər]

It's OK.

Het is okay.
[hɛt is ɔ'kɛj]

It's all right.

Het gaat beter.
[hɛt xāt 'betər]

At the pharmacy

pharmacy (drugstore)	**apotheek** [apɔ'tēk]
24-hour pharmacy	**dag en nacht apotheek** [dax en naxt apɔ'tēk]
Where is the closest pharmacy?	**Waar is de meest nabij gelegen apotheek?** [wār is də mēst na'bɛj xə'lexən apɔ'tēk?]
Is it open now?	**Is hij nu open?** [is hɛj nʉ 'ɔpən?]
At what time does it open?	**Hoe laat gaat hij open?** [hu lāt xāt hɛj 'ɔpən?]
At what time does it close?	**Hoe laat sluit hij?** [hu lāt slœyt hɛj?]
Is it far?	**Is het ver?** [iz ət vɛr?]
Can I get there on foot?	**Kan ik er lopend naar toe?** [kan ik ɛr 'lopənt nār tu?]
Can you show me on the map?	**Kunt u het op de plattegrond aanwijzen?** [kʉnt ju ət ɔp də platə'xrɔnt 'ānwɛjzən?]
Please give me something for ...	**Geef mij alstublieft iets voor ...** [xēf mɛj alstʉ'blift its vōr ...]
a headache	**hoofdpijn** [hōftpɛjn]
a cough	**hoest** [hust]
a cold	**verkoudheid** [vər'kauthɛjt]
the flu	**de griep** [də xrip]
a fever	**koorts** [kōrts]
a stomach ache	**maagpijn** [māxpɛjn]
nausea	**misselijkheid** ['misələkhɛjt]
diarrhea	**diarree** [dia'rē]

constipation	**constipatie** [kɔnsti'patsi]
pain in the back	**rugpijn** [rʉxpɛjn]
chest pain	**pijn in mijn borst** [pɛjn in mɛjn bɔrst]
side stitch	**steek in de zij** [stēk in də zɛj]
abdominal pain	**pijn in mijn onderbuik** [pɛjn in mɛjn 'ɔndərbœʏk]

pill	**pil** [pil]
ointment, cream	**zalf, crème** [zalf, krɛːm]
syrup	**stroop** [strōp]
spray	**verstuiver** [vərstœʏvər]
drops	**druppels** [drʉpəls]

You need to go to the hospital.	**U moet naar het ziekenhuis.** [ju mut nār ət 'zikənhœʏs]
health insurance	**ziektekostenverzekering** [ziktəkɔstən·vər'zekəriŋ]
prescription	**voorschrift** [vōrsxrift]
insect repellant	**anti-insecten middel** [anti-in'sɛktən 'midəl]
Band Aid	**pleister** ['plɛjstər]

The bare minimum

Excuse me, ...	**Pardon, ...** [par'dɔn, ...]
Hello.	**Hallo.** [halɔ]
Thank you.	**Bedankt.** [bə'dankt]
Good bye.	**Tot ziens.** [tɔt zins]
Yes.	**Ja.** [ja]
No.	**Nee.** [nē]
I don't know.	**Ik weet het niet.** [ik wēt ət nit]
Where?	Where to?	When?	**Waar?	Waarheen?	Wanneer?** [wār?	wār'hēn?	wa'nēr?]
I need ...	**Ik heb ... nodig** [ik hɛp ... 'nɔdəx]
I want ...	**Ik wil ...** [ik wil ...]
Do you have ...?	**Hebt u ...?** [hɛpt ju ...?]
Is there a ... here?	**Is hier een ...?** [is hir en ...?]
May I ...?	**Mag ik ...?** [max ik ...?]
..., please (polite request)	**... alstublieft** [... alstʉ'blift]
I'm looking for ...	**Ik zoek ...** [ik zuk ...]
restroom	**toilet** [twa'lɛt]
ATM	**geldautomaat** [xɛlt·autɔ'māt]
pharmacy (drugstore)	**apotheek** [apɔ'tēk]
hospital	**ziekenhuis** [zikənhœys]
police station	**politiebureau** [pɔ\'litsi bʉ\'rɔ]
subway	**metro** ['metrɔ]

taxi	**taxi** [taksi]
train station	**station** [sta'tsjɔn]

My name is ...	**Ik heet ...** [ik hēt ...]
What's your name?	**Hoe heet u?** [hu hēt ju?]
Could you please help me?	**Kunt u me helpen alstublieft?** [kʊnt ju mə 'hɛlpən alstʊ'blift?]
I've got a problem.	**Ik heb een probleem.** [ik hɛp en prɔ'blēm]
I don't feel well.	**Ik voel me niet goed.** [ik vul mə nit xut]
Call an ambulance!	**Bel een ambulance!** [bɛl en ambʊ'lansə!]
May I make a call?	**Mag ik opbellen?** [max ik ɔ'bɛlən?]

I'm sorry.	**Sorry.** ['sɔri]
You're welcome.	**Graag gedaan.** [xrāx xə'dān]

I, me	**Ik, mij** [ik, mɛj]
you (inform.)	**jij** [jɛj]
he	**hij** [hɛj]
she	**zij** [zɛj]
they (masc.)	**zij** [zɛj]
they (fem.)	**zij** [zɛj]
we	**wij** [wɛj]
you (pl)	**jullie** ['juli]
you (sg, form.)	**u** [ju]

ENTRANCE	**INGANG** [inxaŋ]
EXIT	**UITGANG** [œʏtxaŋ]
OUT OF ORDER	**BUITEN GEBRUIK** [bœʏtən xə'brœʏk]
CLOSED	**GESLOTEN** [xə'slɔtən]

OPEN	**OPEN** [ˈɔpən]
FOR WOMEN	**DAMES** [daməs]
FOR MEN	**HEREN** [ˈherən]

T&P BOOKS

CONCISE DICTIONARY

This section contains more than 1,500 useful words arranged alphabetically. The dictionary includes a lot of gastronomic terms and will be helpful when ordering food at a restaurant or buying groceries

T&P Books Publishing

DICTIONARY CONTENTS

T&P Books Publishing

T&P Books Publishing

time	**tijd (de)**	[tɛjt]
hour	**uur (het)**	[ūr]
half an hour	**halfuur (het)**	[half 'ūr]
minute	**minuut (de)**	[mi'nūt]
second	**seconde (de)**	[se'kɔndə]
today (adv)	**vandaag**	[van'dāx]
tomorrow (adv)	**morgen**	['mɔrxən]
yesterday (adv)	**gisteren**	['xistərən]
Monday	**maandag (de)**	['māndax]
Tuesday	**dinsdag (de)**	['dinsdax]
Wednesday	**woensdag (de)**	['wunsdax]
Thursday	**donderdag (de)**	['dɔndərdax]
Friday	**vrijdag (de)**	['vrɛjdax]
Saturday	**zaterdag (de)**	['zatərdax]
Sunday	**zondag (de)**	['zɔndax]
day	**dag (de)**	[dax]
working day	**werkdag (de)**	['wɛrk·dax]
public holiday	**feestdag (de)**	['fēst·dax]
weekend	**weekend (het)**	['wikənt]
week	**week (de)**	[wēk]
last week (adv)	**vorige week**	['vɔrixə wēk]
next week (adv)	**volgende week**	['vɔlxəndə wēk]
sunrise	**zonsopgang (de)**	[zɔns'ɔpxaŋ]
sunset	**zonsondergang (de)**	[zɔns'ɔndərxaŋ]
in the morning	**'s morgens**	[s 'mɔrxəns]
in the afternoon	**'s middags**	[s 'midax]
in the evening	**'s avonds**	[s 'avɔnts]
tonight (this evening)	**vanavond**	[va'navɔnt]
at night	**'s nachts**	[s naxts]
midnight	**middernacht (de)**	['midər·naxt]
January	**januari (de)**	[janʉ'ari]
February	**februari (de)**	[febrʉ'ari]
March	**maart (de)**	[mārt]
April	**april (de)**	[ap'ril]
May	**mei (de)**	[mɛj]
June	**juni (de)**	['juni]

July	juli (de)	['juli]
August	augustus (de)	[au'xʉstʉs]
September	september (de)	[sɛp'tɛmbər]
October	oktober (de)	[ɔk'tɔbər]
November	november (de)	[nɔ'vɛmbər]
December	december (de)	[de'sɛmbər]
in spring	in de lente	[in də 'lɛntə]
in summer	in de zomer	[in də 'zɔmər]
in fall	in de herfst	[in də hɛrfst]
in winter	in de winter	[in də 'wintər]
month	maand (de)	[mānt]
season (summer, etc.)	seizoen (het)	[sɛj'zun]
year	jaar (het)	[jār]
century	eeuw (de)	[ēw]

2. Numbers. Numerals

digit, figure	cijfer (het)	['sɛjfər]
number	nummer (het)	['nʉmər]
minus sign	minteken (het)	['min·tekən]
plus sign	plusteken (het)	['plʉs·tekən]
sum, total	som (de), totaal (het)	[sɔm], [tɔ'tāl]
first (adj)	eerste	['ērstə]
second (adj)	tweede	['twēdə]
third (adj)	derde	['dɛrdə]
0 zero	nul	[nʉl]
1 one	een	[en]
2 two	twee	[twē]
3 three	drie	[dri]
4 four	vier	[vir]
5 five	vijf	[vɛjf]
6 six	zes	[zɛs]
7 seven	zeven	['zevən]
8 eight	acht	[axt]
9 nine	negen	['nexən]
10 ten	tien	[tin]
11 eleven	elf	[ɛlf]
12 twelve	twaalf	[twālf]
13 thirteen	dertien	['dɛrtin]
14 fourteen	veertien	['vērtin]
15 fifteen	vijftien	['vɛjftin]
16 sixteen	zestien	['zɛstin]
17 seventeen	zeventien	['zevəntin]

18 eighteen	**achttien**	['axtin]
19 nineteen	**negentien**	['nexəntin]
20 twenty	**twintig**	['twintəx]
30 thirty	**dertig**	['dɛrtəx]
40 forty	**veertig**	['vērtəx]
50 fifty	**vijftig**	['vɛjftəx]
60 sixty	**zestig**	['zɛstəx]
70 seventy	**zeventig**	['zevəntəx]
80 eighty	**tachtig**	['tahtəx]
90 ninety	**negentig**	['nexəntəx]
100 one hundred	**honderd**	['hondərt]
200 two hundred	**tweehonderd**	[twē·'hondərt]
300 three hundred	**driehonderd**	[dri·'hondərt]
400 four hundred	**vierhonderd**	[vir·'hondərt]
500 five hundred	**vijfhonderd**	[vɛjf·'hondərt]
600 six hundred	**zeshonderd**	[zɛs·'hondərt]
700 seven hundred	**zevenhonderd**	['zevən·'hondərt]
800 eight hundred	**achthonderd**	[axt·'hondərt]
900 nine hundred	**negenhonderd**	['nexən·'hondərt]
1000 one thousand	**duizend**	['dœyzənt]
10000 ten thousand	**tienduizend**	[tin·'dœyzənt]
one hundred thousand	**honderdduizend**	['hondərt·'dœyzənt]
million	**miljoen (het)**	[mi'ljun]
billion	**miljard (het)**	[mi'ljart]

3. Humans. Family

man (adult male)	**man (de)**	[man]
young man	**jongen (de)**	['joŋən]
teenager	**tiener, adolescent (de)**	['tinər], [adɔlɛ'sɛnt]
woman	**vrouw (de)**	['vrau]
girl (young woman)	**meisje (het)**	['mɛjɕə]
age	**leeftijd (de)**	['lēftɛjt]
adult (adj)	**volwassen**	[vɔl'wasən]
middle-aged (adj)	**van middelbare leeftijd**	[van 'midəlbarə 'lēftɛjt]
elderly (adj)	**bejaard**	[bɛ'jārt]
old (adj)	**oud**	['aut]
old man	**oude man (de)**	['audə man]
old woman	**oude vrouw (de)**	['audə 'vrau]
retirement	**pensioen (het)**	[pɛn'ʃun]
to retire (from job)	**met pensioen gaan**	[mɛt pɛn'ʃun xān]
retiree	**gepensioneerde (de)**	[xəpɛnʃə'nērdə]

mother	moeder (de)	['mudər]
father	vader (de)	['vadər]
son	zoon (de)	[zõn]
daughter	dochter (de)	['dɔxtər]
brother	broer (de)	[brur]
elder brother	oudere broer (de)	['audərə brur]
younger brother	jongere broer (de)	['joŋərə brur]
sister	zuster (de)	['zʉstər]
elder sister	oudere zuster (de)	['audərə 'zʉstər]
younger sister	jongere zuster (de)	['joŋərə 'zʉstər]
parents	ouders	['audərs]
child	kind (het)	[kint]
children	kinderen	['kindərən]
stepmother	stiefmoeder (de)	['stif·mudər]
stepfather	stiefvader (de)	['stif·vadər]
grandmother	oma (de)	['ɔma]
grandfather	opa (de)	['ɔpa]
grandson	kleinzoon (de)	[klɛjn·zõn]
granddaughter	kleindochter (de)	[klɛjn·'dɔxtər]
grandchildren	kleinkinderen	[klɛjn·'kindərən]
uncle	oom (de)	[õm]
aunt	tante (de)	['tantə]
nephew	neef (de)	[nẽf]
niece	nicht (de)	[nixt]
wife	vrouw (de)	['vrau]
husband	man (de)	[man]
married (masc.)	gehuwd	[xə'hʉwt]
married (fem.)	gehuwd	[xə'hʉwt]
widow	weduwe (de)	['wedʉwə]
widower	weduwnaar (de)	['wedʉwnãr]
name (first name)	naam (de)	[nãm]
surname (last name)	achternaam (de)	['axtər·nãm]
relative	familielid (het)	[fa'mililit]
friend (masc.)	vriend (de)	[vrint]
friendship	vriendschap (de)	['vrintsxap]
partner	partner (de)	['partnər]
superior (n)	baas (de)	[bãs]
colleague	collega (de)	[kɔ'lexa]
neighbors	buren	['bʉrən]

4. Human body

organism (body)	organisme (het)	[ɔrxa'nismə]
body	lichaam (het)	['lixãm]

heart	hart (het)	[hart]
blood	bloed (het)	[blut]
brain	hersenen	['hɛrsənən]
nerve	zenuw (de)	['zenʉw]

bone	been (het)	[bēn]
skeleton	skelet (het)	[ske'lɛt]
spine (backbone)	ruggengraat (de)	['rʉxə·xrāt]
rib	rib (de)	[rib]
skull	schedel (de)	['sxedəl]

muscle	spier (de)	[spir]
lungs	longen	['lɔŋən]
skin	huid (de)	['hœʏt]

head	hoofd (het)	[hōft]
face	gezicht (het)	[xə'ziht]
nose	neus (de)	['nøs]
forehead	voorhoofd (het)	['vōrhōft]
cheek	wang (de)	[waŋ]

mouth	mond (de)	[mɔnt]
tongue	tong (de)	[tɔŋ]
tooth	tand (de)	[tant]
lips	lippen	['lipən]
chin	kin (de)	[kin]

ear	oor (het)	[ōr]
neck	hals (de)	[hals]
throat	keel (de)	[kēl]

eye	oog (het)	[ōx]
pupil	pupil (de)	[pʉ'pil]
eyebrow	wenkbrauw (de)	['wɛnk·brau]
eyelash	wimper (de)	['wimpər]

hair	haren	['harən]
hairstyle	kapsel (het)	['kapsəl]
mustache	snor (de)	[snɔr]
beard	baard (de)	[bārt]
to have (a beard, etc.)	dragen	['draxən]
bald (adj)	kaal	[kāl]

hand	hand (de)	[hant]
arm	arm (de)	[arm]
finger	vinger (de)	['viŋər]
nail	nagel (de)	['naxəl]
palm	handpalm (de)	['hantpalm]

shoulder	schouder (de)	['sxaudər]
leg	been (het)	[bēn]
foot	voet (de)	[vut]

| knee | knie (de) | [kni] |
| heel | hiel (de) | [hil] |

back	rug (de)	[rʉx]
waist	taille (de)	['tajə]
beauty mark	huidvlek (de)	['hœyt·vlɛk]
birthmark	moedervlek (de)	['mudər·vlɛk]
(café au lait spot)		

5. Medicine. Diseases. Drugs

health	gezondheid (de)	[xə'zɔnthɛjt]
well (not sick)	gezond	[xə'zɔnt]
sickness	ziekte (de)	['ziktə]
to be sick	ziek zijn	[zik zɛjn]
ill, sick (adj)	ziek	[zik]

cold (illness)	verkoudheid (de)	[vər'kauthɛjt]
to catch a cold	verkouden raken	[vər'kaudən 'rakən]
tonsillitis	angina (de)	[an'xina]
pneumonia	longontsteking (de)	['lɔŋ·ɔntstekiŋ]
flu, influenza	griep (de)	[xrip]

runny nose (coryza)	snotneus (de)	[snɔt'nøs]
cough	hoest (de)	[hust]
to cough (vi)	hoesten	['hustən]
to sneeze (vi)	niezen	['nizən]

stroke	beroerte (de)	[bə'rurtə]
heart attack	hartinfarct (het)	['hart·in'farkt]
allergy	allergie (de)	[alɛr'xi]
asthma	astma (de/het)	['astma]
diabetes	diabetes (de)	[dia'betəs]

tumor	tumor (de)	['tʉmɔr]
cancer	kanker (de)	['kankər]
alcoholism	alcoholisme (het)	[alkɔhɔ'lismə]
AIDS	AIDS (de)	[ets]
fever	koorts (de)	[kõrts]
seasickness	zeeziekte (de)	[zē·'ziktə]

bruise (hématome)	blauwe plek (de)	['blauə plɛk]
bump (lump)	buil (de)	['bœyl]
to limp (vi)	hinken	['hinkən]
dislocation	verstuiking (de)	[vər'stœɣkiŋ]
to dislocate (vt)	verstuiken	[vər'stœɣkən]

fracture	breuk (de)	['brøk]
burn (injury)	brandwond (de)	['brant·wont]
injury	blessure (de)	[blɛ'sʉrə]

pain, ache	**pijn (de)**	[pɛjn]
toothache	**tandpijn (de)**	['tand·pɛjn]
to sweat (perspire)	**zweten**	['zwetən]
deaf (adj)	**doof**	[dõf]
mute (adj)	**stom**	[stɔm]
immunity	**immuniteit (de)**	[imʉni'tɛjt]
virus	**virus (het)**	['virʉs]
microbe	**microbe (de)**	[mik'rɔbə]
bacterium	**bacterie (de)**	[bak'teri]
infection	**infectie (de)**	[in'fɛksi]
hospital	**ziekenhuis (het)**	['zikən·hœʏs]
cure	**genezing (de)**	[xə'neziŋ]
to vaccinate (vt)	**inenten**	['inɛntən]
to be in a coma	**in coma liggen**	[in 'kɔma 'lixən]
intensive care	**intensieve zorg, ICU (de)**	[intən'sivə zɔrx], [isɛ'ju]
symptom	**symptoom (het)**	[simp'tõm]
pulse	**polsslag (de)**	['pɔls·slax]

6. Feelings. Emotions. Conversation

I, me	**ik**	[ik]
you	**jij, je**	[jɛj], [jə]
he	**hij**	[hɛj]
she	**zij, ze**	[zɛj], [zə]
it	**het**	[ət]
we	**wij, we**	[wɛj], [wə]
you (to a group)	**jullie**	['juli]
they	**zij, ze**	[zɛj], [zə]
Hello! (fam.)	**Hallo! Dag!**	[ha'lɔ dax]
Hello! (form.)	**Hallo!**	[ha'lɔ]
Good morning!	**Goedemorgen!**	['xudə·'mɔrxən]
Good afternoon!	**Goedemiddag!**	['xudə·'midax]
Good evening!	**Goedenavond!**	['xudən·'avɔnt]
to say hello	**gedag zeggen**	[xe'dax 'zexən]
to greet (vt)	**verwelkomen**	[vər'wɛlkɔmən]
How are you?	**Hoe gaat het?**	[hu xãt ət]
Goodbye!	**Tot ziens!**	[tɔt 'tsins]
Bye!	**Doei!**	['dui]
Thank you!	**Dank u!**	[dank ju]
feelings	**gevoelens**	[xə'vuləns]
to be hungry	**honger hebben**	['hɔŋər 'hɛbən]
to be thirsty	**dorst hebben**	[dɔrst 'hɛbən]
tired (adj)	**moe**	[mu]

to be worried	bezorgd zijn	[bə'zɔrxt zɛjn]
to be nervous	zenuwachtig zijn	['zenɵw·ahtəx zɛjn]
hope	hoop (de)	[hōp]
to hope (vi, vt)	hopen	['hɔpən]
character	karakter (het)	[ka'raktər]
modest (adj)	bescheiden	[bə'sxɛjdən]
lazy (adj)	lui	['lœɣ]
generous (adj)	gul	[xjul]
talented (adj)	talentrijk	[ta'lɛntrɛjk]
honest (adj)	eerlijk	['ērlək]
serious (adj)	ernstig	['ɛrnstəx]
shy, timid (adj)	schuchter	['sxɵxtər]
sincere (adj)	oprecht	[ɔp'rɛxt]
coward	lafaard (de)	['lafārt]
to sleep (vi)	slapen	['slapən]
dream	droom (de)	[drōm]
bed	bed (het)	[bɛt]
pillow	kussen (het)	['kɵsən]
insomnia	slapeloosheid (de)	['slapəlōshɛjt]
to go to bed	gaan slapen	[xān 'slapən]
nightmare	nachtmerrie (de)	['naxtmɛri]
alarm clock	wekker (de)	['wɛkər]
smile	glimlach (de)	['xlimlah]
to smile (vi)	glimlachen	['xlimlahən]
to laugh (vi)	lachen	['laxən]
quarrel	ruzie (de)	['rɵzi]
insult	belediging (de)	[bə'ledəxiŋ]
resentment	krenking (de)	['krenkiŋ]
angry (mad)	boos	[bōs]

7. Clothing. Personal accessories

clothes	kleren (mv.)	['klerən]
coat (overcoat)	jas (de)	[jas]
fur coat	bontjas (de)	[bɔnt jas]
jacket (e.g., leather ~)	jasje (het)	['jaɕə]
raincoat (trenchcoat, etc.)	regenjas (de)	['rexən jas]
shirt (button shirt)	overhemd (het)	['ɔvərhɛmt]
pants	broek (de)	[bruk]
suit jacket	colbert (de)	['kɔlbər]
suit	kostuum (het)	[kɔs'tūm]
dress (frock)	jurk (de)	[jurk]
skirt	rok (de)	[rɔk]

T-shirt	**T-shirt (het)**	['tiʃøt]
bathrobe	**badjas (de)**	['batjas]
pajamas	**pyjama (de)**	[pi'jama]
workwear	**werkkleding (de)**	['wɛrk·'klediŋ]
underwear	**ondergoed (het)**	['ɔndərxut]
socks	**sokken**	['sɔkən]
bra	**beha (de)**	[be'ha]
pantyhose	**panty (de)**	['pɛnti]
stockings (thigh highs)	**nylonkousen**	['nɛjlɔn·'kausən]
bathing suit	**badpak (het)**	['bad·pak]
hat	**hoed (de)**	[hut]
footwear	**schoeisel (het)**	['sxuisəl]
boots (e.g., cowboy ~)	**laarzen**	['lãrzən]
heel	**hiel (de)**	[hil]
shoestring	**veter (de)**	['vetər]
shoe polish	**schoensmeer (de/het)**	['sxun·smēr]
cotton (n)	**katoen (de/het)**	[ka'tun]
wool (n)	**wol (de)**	[wɔl]
fur (n)	**bont (het)**	[bɔnt]
gloves	**handschoenen**	['xand 'sxunən]
mittens	**wanten**	['wantən]
scarf (muffler)	**sjaal (de)**	[çãl]
glasses (eyeglasses)	**bril (de)**	[bril]
umbrella	**paraplu (de)**	[parap'lʉ]
tie (necktie)	**das (de)**	[das]
handkerchief	**zakdoek (de)**	['zagduk]
comb	**kam (de)**	[kam]
hairbrush	**haarborstel (de)**	[hãr·'bɔrstəl]
buckle	**gesp (de)**	[xɛsp]
belt	**broekriem (de)**	['bruk·rim]
purse	**damestas (de)**	['daməs·tas]
collar	**kraag (de)**	[krãx]
pocket	**zak (de)**	[zak]
sleeve	**mouw (de)**	['mau]
fly (on trousers)	**gulp (de)**	[xjulp]
zipper (fastener)	**rits (de)**	[rits]
button	**knoop (de)**	[knõp]
to get dirty (vi)	**vies worden**	[vis 'wɔrdən]
stain (mark, spot)	**vlek (de)**	[vlɛk]

8. City. Urban institutions

store	**winkel (de)**	['winkəl]
shopping mall	**winkelcentrum (het)**	['winkəl·'sɛntrʉm]

supermarket	supermarkt (de)	['sʉpərmarkt]
shoe store	schoenwinkel (de)	['sxun·'winkəl]
bookstore	boekhandel (de)	['bukən·'handəl]

drugstore, pharmacy	apotheek (de)	[apɔ'tēk]
bakery	bakkerij (de)	['bakərɛj]
pastry shop	banketbakkerij (de)	[ban'ket·bakə'rɛj]
grocery store	kruidenier (de)	[krœydə'nir]
butcher shop	slagerij (de)	[slaxə'rɛj]
produce store	groentewinkel (de)	['xruntə·'winkəl]
market	markt (de)	[markt]

hair salon	kapperssalon (de/het)	['kapərs·sa'lɔn]
post office	postkantoor (het)	[pɔst·kan'tõr]
dry cleaners	stomerij (de)	[stɔmɛ'rɛj]
circus	circus (de/het)	['sirkʉs]
zoo	dierentuin (de)	['dīrən·tœyn]

theater	theater (het)	[te'atər]
movie theater	bioscoop (de)	[biɔ'skōp]
museum	museum (het)	[mʉ'zejum]
library	bibliotheek (de)	[biblɪɔ'tēk]

mosque	moskee (de)	[mɔs'kē]
synagogue	synagoge (de)	[sina'xɔxə]
cathedral	kathedraal (de)	[kate'drāl]
temple	tempel (de)	['tɛmpəl]
church	kerk (de)	[kɛrk]

college	instituut (het)	[insti'tūt]
university	universiteit (de)	[junivɛrsi'tɛjt]
school	school (de)	[sxōl]

hotel	hotel (het)	[hɔ'tɛl]
bank	bank (de)	[bank]
embassy	ambassade (de)	[amba'sadə]
travel agency	reisbureau (het)	[rɛjs·bʉ'rɔ]

subway	metro (de)	['metrɔ]
hospital	ziekenhuis (het)	['zikən·hœys]
gas station	benzinestation (het)	[bɛn'zinə·sta'tsjɔn]
parking lot	parking (de)	['parkiŋ]

ENTRANCE	INGANG	['inxaŋ]
EXIT	UITGANG	['œytxaŋ]
PUSH	DUWEN	['dʉwən]
PULL	TREKKEN	['trɛkən]
OPEN	OPEN	['ɔpən]
CLOSED	GESLOTEN	[xə'slɔtən]

| monument | monument (het) | [mɔnʉ'mɛnt] |
| fortress | vesting (de) | ['vɛstiŋ] |

palace	paleis (het)	[pa'lɛjs]
medieval (adj)	middeleeuws	['midǝlēws]
ancient (adj)	oud	['aut]
national (adj)	nationaal	[natsjɔ'nāl]
famous (monument, etc.)	bekend	[bǝ'kɛnt]

9. Money. Finances

money	geld (het)	[xɛlt]
coin	muntstuk (de)	['mʉntstʉk]
dollar	dollar (de)	['dɔlar]
euro	euro (de)	[ørɔ]

ATM	geldautomaat (de)	[xɛlt·auto'māt]
currency exchange	wisselkantoor (het)	['wisǝl·kan'tōr]
exchange rate	koers (de)	[kurs]
cash	baar geld (het)	[bār 'xɛlt]

How much?	Hoeveel?	[hu'vēl]
to pay (vi, vt)	betalen	[bǝ'talǝn]
payment	betaling (de)	[bǝ'taliŋ]
change (give the ~)	wisselgeld (het)	['wisǝl·xɛlt]

price	prijs (de)	[prɛjs]
discount	korting (de)	['kɔrtiŋ]
cheap (adj)	goedkoop	[xut'kōp]
expensive (adj)	duur	[dūr]

bank	bank (de)	[bank]
account	bankrekening (de)	[bank·'rekǝniŋ]
credit card	kredietkaart (de)	[kre'dit·kārt]
check	cheque (de)	[ʃɛk]
to write a check	een cheque uitschrijven	[en ʃɛk œyt'sxrɛjvǝn]
checkbook	chequeboekje (het)	[ʃɛk·'bukjǝ]

debt	schuld (de)	[sxʉlt]
debtor	schuldenaar (de)	['sxʉldǝnār]
to lend (money)	uitlenen	['œytlǝnǝn]
to borrow (vi, vt)	lenen	['lenǝn]

to rent (~ a tuxedo)	huren	['hʉrǝn]
on credit (adv)	op krediet	[ɔp kre'dit]
wallet	portefeuille (de)	[pɔrtǝ'fœyǝ]
safe	safe (de)	[sef]
inheritance	erfenis (de)	['ɛrfǝnis]
fortune (wealth)	fortuin (het)	[fɔr'tœyn]

tax	belasting (de)	[bǝ'lastiŋ]
fine	boete (de)	['butǝ]
to fine (vt)	beboeten	[bǝ'butǝn]

wholesale (adj)	groothandels-	[xrōt·'handəls]
retail (adj)	kleinhandels-	[klɛjn·'handəls]
to insure (vt)	verzekeren	[vər'zekərən]
insurance	verzekering (de)	[vər'zekəriŋ]

capital	kapitaal (het)	[kapi'tāl]
turnover	omzet (de)	['ɔmzɛt]
stock (share)	aandeel (het)	['āndēl]
profit	winst (de)	[winst]
profitable (adj)	winstgevend	[winst'xevənt]

crisis	crisis (de)	['krisis]
bankruptcy	bankroet (het)	[bank'rut]
to go bankrupt	bankroet gaan	[bank'rut xān]

accountant	boekhouder (de)	[buk 'haudər]
salary	salaris (het)	[sa'laris]
bonus (money)	premie (de)	['premi]

10. Transportation

bus	bus, autobus (de)	[bʉs], ['autobʉs]
streetcar	tram (de)	[trɛm]
trolley bus	trolleybus (de)	['trɔlibʉs]

to go by ...	rijden met ...	['rɛjdən mɛt]
to get on (~ the bus)	stappen	['stapən]
to get off ...	afstappen	['afstapən]

stop (e.g., bus ~)	halte (de)	['haltə]
terminus	eindpunt (het)	['ɛjnt·pʉnt]
schedule	dienstregeling (de)	[dinst·'rexəliŋ]
ticket	kaartje (het)	['kārtʃə]
to be late (for ...)	te laat zijn	[tə 'lāt zɛjn]

taxi, cab	taxi (de)	['taksi]
by taxi	met de taxi	[mɛt də 'taksi]
taxi stand	taxistandplaats (de)	['taksi·'stant·plāts]

traffic	verkeer (het)	[vər'kēr]
rush hour	spitsuur (het)	['spits·ūr]
to park (vi)	parkeren	[par'kerən]

subway	metro (de)	['metrɔ]
station	halte (de)	['haltə]
train	trein (de)	[trɛjn]
train station	station (het)	[sta'tsjon]
rails	rails	['rɛjls]
compartment	coupé (de)	[ku'pɛ]
berth	bed (het)	[bɛt]

airplane	**vliegtuig (het)**	['vlixtœʏx]
air ticket	**vliegticket (het)**	['vlix·'tikət]
airline	**luchtvaart-**	['lʉxtvɑrt
	maatschappij (de)	mɑtsxa'pɛj]
airport	**luchthaven (de)**	['lʉxthavən]
flight (act of flying)	**vlucht (de)**	[vlʉxt]
luggage	**bagage (de)**	[ba'xaʒə]
luggage cart	**bagagekarretje (het)**	[ba'xaʒə·'karɛtʃə]
ship	**schip (het)**	[sxip]
cruise ship	**lijnschip (het)**	['lɛjn·sxip]
yacht	**jacht (het)**	[jɑxt]
boat (flat-bottomed ~)	**boot (de)**	[bõt]
captain	**kapitein (de)**	[kapi'tɛjn]
cabin	**kajuit (de)**	[kajœʏt]
port (harbor)	**haven (de)**	['havən]
bicycle	**fiets (de)**	[fits]
scooter	**bromfiets (de)**	['brɔmfits]
motorcycle, bike	**motorfiets (de)**	['mɔtɔrfits]
pedal	**pedaal (de/het)**	[pe'dãl]
pump	**pomp (de)**	[pɔmp]
wheel	**wiel (het)**	[wil]
automobile, car	**auto (de)**	['autɔ]
ambulance	**ambulance (de)**	[ambʉ'lansə]
truck	**vrachtwagen (de)**	['vrɑht·'waxən]
used (adj)	**tweedehands**	[twẽdə'hants]
car crash	**auto-ongeval (het)**	['autɔ-'ɔŋɛval]
repair	**reparatie (de)**	[repa'ratsi]

11. Food. Part 1

meat	**vlees (het)**	[vlẽs]
chicken	**kip (de)**	[kip]
duck	**eend (de)**	[ẽnt]
pork	**varkensvlees (het)**	['varkəns·vlẽs]
veal	**kalfsvlees (het)**	['kalfs·vlẽs]
lamb	**schapenvlees (het)**	['sxapən·vlẽs]
beef	**rundvlees (het)**	['rʉnt·vlẽs]
sausage (bologna, pepperoni, etc.)	**worst (de)**	[wɔrst]
egg	**ei (het)**	[ɛj]
fish	**vis (de)**	[vis]
cheese	**kaas (de)**	[kãs]
sugar	**suiker (de)**	[sœʏkər]

salt	zout (het)	['zɑut]
rice	rijst (de)	[rɛjst]
pasta (macaroni)	pasta (de)	['pasta]
butter	boter (de)	['botər]
vegetable oil	plantaardige olie (de)	[plant'ārdixə 'ɔli]
bread	brood (het)	[brōt]
chocolate (n)	chocolade (de)	[ʃɔkɔ'ladə]
wine	wijn (de)	[wɛjn]
coffee	koffie (de)	['kɔfi]
milk	melk (de)	[mɛlk]
juice	sap (het)	[sap]
beer	bier (het)	[bir]
tea	thee (de)	[tē]
tomato	tomaat (de)	[tɔ'māt]
cucumber	augurk (de)	[au'xʉrk]
carrot	wortel (de)	['wɔrtəl]
potato	aardappel (de)	['ārd·apəl]
onion	ui (de)	['œy]
garlic	knoflook (de)	['knōflɔk]
cabbage	kool (de)	[kōl]
beetroot	rode biet (de)	['rɔdə bit]
eggplant	aubergine (de)	[ɔbɛr'ʒinə]
dill	dille (de)	['dilə]
lettuce	sla (de)	[sla]
corn (maize)	maïs (de)	[majs]
fruit	vrucht (de)	[vrʉxt]
apple	appel (de)	['apəl]
pear	peer (de)	[pēr]
lemon	citroen (de)	[si'trun]
orange	sinaasappel (de)	['sināsapəl]
strawberry (garden ~)	aardbei (de)	['ārd·bɛj]
plum	pruim (de)	['prœʏm]
raspberry	framboos (de)	[fram'bōs]
pineapple	ananas (de)	['ananas]
banana	banaan (de)	[ba'nān]
watermelon	watermeloen (de)	['watərmɛ'lun]
grape	druif (de)	[drœʏf]
melon	meloen (de)	[mə'lun]

12. Food. Part 2

cuisine	keuken (de)	['køkən]
recipe	recept (het)	[re'sɛpt]
food	eten (het)	['etən]
to have breakfast	ontbijten	[ɔn'bɛjtən]

| to have lunch | lunchen | ['lʉnʃən] |
| to have dinner | souperen | [su'perən] |

taste, flavor	smaak (de)	[smāk]
tasty (adj)	lekker	['lɛkər]
cold (adj)	koud	['kaut]
hot (adj)	heet	[hēt]
sweet (sugary)	zoet	[zut]
salty (adj)	gezouten	[xə'zautən]

sandwich (bread)	boterham (de)	['botərham]
side dish	garnering (de)	[xar'neriŋ]
filling (for cake, pie)	vulling (de)	['vʉliŋ]
sauce	saus (de)	['saus]
piece (of cake, pie)	stuk (het)	[stʉk]

diet	dieet (het)	[di'ēt]
vitamin	vitamine (de)	[vita'minə]
calorie	calorie (de)	[kalɔ'ri]
vegetarian (n)	vegetariër (de)	[vəxɛ'tarier]

restaurant	restaurant (het)	[rɛstɔ'rant]
coffee house	koffiehuis (het)	['kɔfi·hœʏs]
appetite	eetlust (de)	['ētlʉst]
Enjoy your meal!	Eet smakelijk!	[ēt 'smakələk]

waiter	kelner, ober (de)	['kɛlnər], ['ɔbər]
waitress	serveerster (de)	[sɛr'vērstər]
bartender	barman (de)	['barman]
menu	menu (het)	[me'nʉ]

spoon	lepel (de)	['lepəl]
knife	mes (het)	[mɛs]
fork	vork (de)	[vɔrk]
cup (e.g., coffee ~)	kopje (het)	['kɔpjə]

plate (dinner ~)	bord (het)	[bɔrt]
saucer	schoteltje (het)	['sxɔtɛltʃə]
napkin (on table)	servet (het)	[sɛr'vɛt]
toothpick	tandenstoker (de)	['tandən·'stɔkər]

to order (meal)	bestellen	[bə'stɛlən]
course, dish	gerecht (het)	[xe'rɛht]
portion	portie (de)	['pɔrsi]
appetizer	voorgerecht (het)	['vōrxərɛht]
salad	salade (de)	[sa'ladə]
soup	soep (de)	[sup]

dessert	dessert (het)	[dɛ'sɛːr]
jam (whole fruit jam)	confituur (de)	[kɔnfi'tūr]
ice-cream	ijsje (het)	['ɛisjə], ['ɛiʃə]
check	rekening (de)	['rekəniŋ]

| to pay the check | de rekening betalen | [də 'rekəniŋ bə'talən] |
| tip | fooi (de) | [fōj] |

13. House. Apartment. Part 1

house	huis (het)	['hœys]
country house	landhuisje (het)	['lant·hœyɣə]
villa (seaside ~)	villa (de)	['vila]
floor, story	verdieping (de)	[vər'dipiŋ]
entrance	ingang (de)	['inxaŋ]
wall	muur (de)	[mūr]
roof	dak (het)	[dak]
chimney	schoorsteen (de)	['sxōr·stēn]
attic (storage place)	zolder (de)	['zɔldər]
window	venster (het)	['vɛnstər]
window ledge	vensterbank (de)	['vɛnstər·bank]
balcony	balkon (het)	[bal'kɔn]
stairs (stairway)	trap (de)	[trap]
mailbox	postbus (de)	['post·bʉs]
garbage can	vuilnisbak (de)	['vœylnis·bak]
elevator	lift (de)	[lift]
electricity	elektriciteit (de)	[ɛlɛktrisi'tɛjt]
light bulb	lamp (de)	[lamp]
switch	schakelaar (de)	['sxakəlār]
wall socket	stopcontact (het)	['stɔp·kɔn'takt]
fuse	zekering (de)	['zekəriŋ]
door	deur (de)	['dør]
handle, doorknob	deurkruk (de)	['dør·krʉk]
key	sleutel (de)	['sløtəl]
doormat	deurmat (de)	['dør·mat]
door lock	slot (het)	[slɔt]
doorbell	deurbel (de)	['dør·bel]
knock (at the door)	geklop (het)	[xə'klɔp]
to knock (vi)	kloppen	['klɔpən]
peephole	deurspion (de)	['dør·spiɔn]
yard	cour (de)	[kur]
garden	tuin (de)	['tœyn]
swimming pool	zwembad (het)	['zwɛm·bat]
gym (home gym)	gym (het)	[ʒim]
tennis court	tennisveld (het)	['tɛnis·vɛlt]
garage	garage (de)	[xa'raʒə]
private property	privé-eigendom (het)	[pri've-'ɛjxəndɔm]
warning sign	waarschuwings-bord (het)	['wārsxjuviŋs bɔrt]

| security | bewaking (de) | [bə'wakiŋ] |
| security guard | bewaker (de) | [bə'wakər] |

renovations	renovatie (de)	[renɔ'vatsi]
to renovate (vt)	renoveren	[renɔ'virən]
to put in order	op orde brengen	[ɔp 'ɔrdə 'brɛŋən]
to paint (~ a wall)	verven	['vɛrvən]
wallpaper	behang (het)	[bə'haŋ]
to varnish (vt)	lakken	['lakən]

pipe	buis, leiding (de)	['bœys], ['lɛjdiŋ]
tools	gereedschap (het)	[xə'rētsxap]
basement	kelder (de)	['kɛldər]
sewerage (system)	riolering (de)	[riɔ'lɛriŋ]

14. House. Apartment. Part 2

apartment	appartement (het)	[apartə'mɛnt]
room	kamer (de)	['kamər]
bedroom	slaapkamer (de)	['slāp·kamər]
dining room	eetkamer (de)	[ēt·'kamər]

living room	salon (de)	[sa'lɔn]
study (home office)	studeerkamer (de)	[stu'dēr·'kamər]
entry room	gang (de)	[xaŋ]
bathroom (room with a bath or shower)	badkamer (de)	['bat·kamər]
half bath	toilet (het)	[tua'lɛt]

| floor | vloer (de) | [vlur] |
| ceiling | plafond (het) | [pla'fɔnt] |

to dust (vt)	stoffen	['stɔfən]
vacuum cleaner	stofzuiger (de)	['stɔf·zœyxər]
to vacuum (vt)	stofzuigen	['stɔf·zœyxən]

mop	zwabber (de)	['zwabər]
dust cloth	poetsdoek (de)	['putsduk]
short broom	veger (de)	['vexər]
dustpan	stofblik (het)	['stɔf·blik]

furniture	meubels	['møbəl]
table	tafel (de)	['tafəl]
chair	stoel (de)	[stul]
armchair	fauteuil (de)	[fɔ'tøj]

bookcase	boekenkast (de)	['bukən·kast]
shelf	boekenrek (het)	['bukən·rɛk]
wardrobe	kledingkast (de)	['klediŋ·kast]
mirror	spiegel (de)	['spixəl]

carpet	tapijt (het)	[ta'pɛjt]
fireplace	haard (de)	[hãrt]
drapes	gordijnen	[xɔr'dɛjnən]
table lamp	bureaulamp (de)	[bʉ'rɔ·lamp]
chandelier	luchter (de)	['lʉxtər]
kitchen	keuken (de)	['køkən]
gas stove (range)	gasfornuis (het)	[xas·fɔr'nœys]
electric stove	elektrisch fornuis (het)	[ɛ'lɛktris fɔr'nœys]
microwave oven	magnetronoven (de)	['mahnətrɔn·'ɔvən]
refrigerator	koelkast (de)	['kul·kast]
freezer	diepvriezer (de)	[dip·'vrizər]
dishwasher	vaatwasmachine (de)	['vãtwas·ma'ʃinə]
faucet	kraan (de)	[krãn]
meat grinder	vleesmolen (de)	['vlēs·mɔlən]
juicer	vruchtenpers (de)	['vrʉxtən·pɛrs]
toaster	toaster (de)	['tõstər]
mixer	mixer (de)	['miksər]
coffee machine	koffiemachine (de)	['kɔfi·ma'ʃinə]
kettle	fluitketel (de)	['flœyt·'ketəl]
teapot	theepot (de)	['tē·pɔt]
TV set	televisie (de)	[telə'vizi]
VCR (video recorder)	videorecorder (de)	['videɔ·re'kɔrdər]
iron (e.g., steam ~)	strijkijzer (het)	['strɛjk·ɛjzər]
telephone	telefoon (de)	[telə'fõn]

15. Professions. Social status

director	directeur (de)	[dirɛk'tør]
superior	baas (de)	[bãs]
president	president (de)	[prezi'dɛnt]
assistant	assistent (de)	[asi'stɛnt]
secretary	secretaris (de)	[sekre'taris]
owner, proprietor	eigenaar (de)	['ɛjxənãr]
partner	partner (de)	['partnər]
stockholder	aandeelhouder (de)	['ãndēl·haudər]
businessman	zakenman (de)	['zakənman]
millionaire	miljonair (de)	[milju'nɛ:r]
billionaire	miljardair (de)	[miljar'dɛ:r]
actor	acteur (de)	[ak'tør]
architect	architect (de)	[arʃi'tɛkt]
banker	bankier (de)	[baŋ'kir]
broker	makelaar (de)	['makəlãr]

veterinarian	dierenarts (de)	['dīrən·arts]
doctor	dokter, arts (de)	['doktər], [arts]
chambermaid	kamermeisje (het)	['kamər·'mɛjɕə]
designer	designer (de)	[di'zajnər]
correspondent	correspondent (de)	[kɔrɛspɔn'dɛnt]
delivery man	koerier (de)	[ku'rir]

electrician	elektricien (de)	[ɛlɛktri'sjen]
musician	muzikant (de)	[muzi'kant]
babysitter	babysitter (de)	['bɛjbisitər]
hairdresser	kapper (de)	['kapər]
herder, shepherd	herder (de)	['hɛrdər]

singer (masc.)	zanger (de)	['zaŋər]
translator	vertaler (de)	[vər'talər]
writer	schrijver (de)	['sxrɛjvər]
carpenter	timmerman (de)	['timərman]
cook	kok (de)	[kɔk]

fireman	brandweerman (de)	['brantwēr·man]
police officer	politieagent (de)	[po'litsi·a'xɛnt]
mailman	postbode (de)	['pɔst·bodə]
programmer	programmeur (de)	[prɔxra'mør]
salesman (store staff)	verkoper (de)	[vər'kɔpər]

worker	arbeider (de)	['arbɛjdər]
gardener	tuinman (de)	['tœyn·man]
plumber	loodgieter (de)	['lōtxitər]
dentist	tandarts (de)	['tand·arts]
flight attendant (fem.)	stewardess (de)	[stʉwər'dɛs]

dancer (masc.)	danser (de)	['dansər]
bodyguard	lijfwacht (de)	['lɛjf·waxt]
scientist	wetenschapper (de)	['wetənsxapər]
schoolteacher	meester (de)	['mēstər]

farmer	landbouwer (de)	['lantbauər]
surgeon	chirurg (de)	[ʃi'rʉrx]
miner	mijnwerker (de)	['mɛjn·wɛrkər]
chef (kitchen chef)	chef-kok (de)	[ʃɛf-'kɔk]
driver	chauffeur (de)	[ʃɔ'før]

16. Sport

kind of sports	soort sport (de/het)	[sōrt spɔrt]
soccer	voetbal (het)	['vutbal]
hockey	hockey (het)	['hɔki]
basketball	basketbal (het)	['bāskətbal]
baseball	baseball (het)	['bejzbɔl]
volleyball	volleybal (het)	['vɔlibal]

boxing	**boksen (het)**	['bɔksən]
wrestling	**worstelen (het)**	['wɔrstələn]
tennis	**tennis (het)**	['tɛnis]
swimming	**zwemmen (het)**	['zwɛmən]

chess	**schaak (het)**	[sxāk]
running	**hardlopen (het)**	['hardlɔpən]
athletics	**atletiek (de)**	[atle'tik]
figure skating	**kunstschaatsen (het)**	['kʉnst·'sxātsən]
cycling	**wielersport (de)**	['wilər·spɔrt]

billiards	**biljart (het)**	[bi'ljart]
bodybuilding	**bodybuilding (de)**	[bɔdi·'bildiŋ]
golf	**golf (het)**	[gɔlf]
scuba diving	**duiken (het)**	['dœʏkən]
sailing	**zeilen (het)**	['zɛjlən]
archery	**boogschieten (het)**	['bōx·'sxitən]

period, half	**helft (de)**	[hɛlft]
half-time	**pauze (de)**	['pauzə]
tie	**gelijkspel (het)**	[xə'lɛjk·spɛl]
to tie (vi)	**in gelijk spel eindigen**	[in xə'lɛjk spɛl 'ɛjndixən]

treadmill	**loopband (de)**	['lōp·bant]
player	**speler (de)**	['spelər]
substitute	**reservespeler (de)**	[re'zɛrvə·'spelər]
substitutes bench	**reservebank (de)**	[re'zɛrvə·bank]
match	**match, wedstrijd (de)**	[matʃ], ['wɛtstrɛjt]
goal	**doel (het)**	[dul]
goalkeeper	**doelman (de)**	['dulman]
goal (score)	**goal (de)**	[gōl]

Olympic Games	**Olympische Spelen**	[ɔ'limpisə 'spelən]
to set a record	**een record breken**	[ən re'kɔr 'brekən]
final	**finale (de)**	[fi'nalə]
champion	**kampioen (de)**	[kam'pjun]
championship	**kampioenschap (het)**	[kam'pjunsxap]

winner	**winnaar (de)**	['winār]
victory	**overwinning (de)**	[ɔvər'winiŋ]
to win (vi)	**winnen**	['winən]
to lose (not win)	**verliezen**	[vər'lizən]
medal	**medaille (de)**	[me'dajə]

first place	**eerste plaats (de)**	['ērstə plāts]
second place	**tweede plaats (de)**	['twēdə plāts]
third place	**derde plaats (de)**	['dɛrdə plāts]

stadium	**stadion (het)**	[stadi'ɔn]
fan, supporter	**fan, supporter (de)**	[fan], [sʉ'pɔrtər]
trainer, coach	**trainer, coach (de)**	['trɛnər], [kɔtʃ]
training	**training (de)**	['trɛjniŋ]

95

17. Foreign languages. Orthography

language	taal (de)	[tãl]
to study (vt)	leren	['lerən]
pronunciation	uitspraak (de)	['œʏtsprãk]
accent	accent (het)	[ak'sɛnt]
noun	zelfstandig naamwoord (het)	[zɛlf'standix 'nãmwõrt]
adjective	bijvoeglijk naamwoord (het)	[bɛj'fuxlək 'nãmwõrt]
verb	werkwoord (het)	['wɛrk·vɔrt]
adverb	bijwoord (het)	['bɛj·wõrt]
pronoun	voornaamwoord (het)	['võrnãm·wõrt]
interjection	tussenwerpsel (het)	['tʉsən·'wɛrpsəl]
preposition	voorzetsel (het)	['võrzɛtsəl]
root	stam (de)	[stam]
ending	achtervoegsel (het)	['axtər·vuxsəl]
prefix	voorvoegsel (het)	['võr·vuxsəl]
syllable	lettergreep (de)	['lɛtər·xrẽp]
suffix	achtervoegsel (het)	['axtər·vuxsəl]
stress mark	nadruk (de)	['nadrʉk]
period, dot	punt (de)	[pʉnt]
comma	komma (de/het)	['kɔma]
colon	dubbelpunt (de)	['dʉbəl·pʉnt]
ellipsis	beletselteken (het)	[bə'lɛtsel·'tekən]
question	vraag (de)	[vrãx]
question mark	vraagteken (het)	['vrãx·tekən]
exclamation point	uitroepteken (het)	['œʏtrup·tekən]
in quotation marks	tussen aanhalingstekens	['tʉsən 'ãnhaliŋ's·tekəns]
in parenthesis	tussen haakjes	['tʉsən 'hãkjəs]
letter	letter (de)	['lɛtər]
capital letter	hoofdletter (de)	[hõft·'lɛtər]
sentence	zin (de)	[zin]
group of words	woordgroep (de)	['wõrt·xrup]
expression	uitdrukking (de)	['œʏdrykiŋ]
subject	onderwerp (het)	['ɔndərwɛrp]
predicate	gezegde (het)	[xə'zɛxdə]
line	regel (de)	['rexəl]
paragraph	alinea (de)	[a'linɛa]
synonym	synoniem (het)	[sinɔ'nim]
antonym	antoniem (het)	[antɔ'nim]
exception	uitzondering (de)	['œʏtzɔndəriŋ]

to underline (vt)	onderstrepen	['ɔndər'strepən]
rules	regels	['rexəls]
grammar	grammatica (de)	[xra'matika]
vocabulary	vocabulaire (het)	[vɔkabʉ'lɛːr]
phonetics	fonetiek (de)	[fɔnɛ'tik]
alphabet	alfabet (het)	['alfabət]

textbook	leerboek (het)	['lēr·buk]
dictionary	woordenboek (het)	['wōrdən·buk]
phrasebook	taalgids (de)	['tāl·xits]

word	woord (het)	[wōrt]
meaning	betekenis (de)	[bə'tekənis]
memory	geheugen (het)	[xə'høxən]

18. The Earth. Geography

the Earth	Aarde (de)	['ārdə]
the globe (the Earth)	aardbol (de)	['ārd·bol]
planet	planeet (de)	[pla'nēt]

geography	aardrijkskunde (de)	['ārdrɛjkskʉndə]
nature	natuur (de)	[na'tūr]
map	kaart (de)	[kārt]
atlas	atlas (de)	['atlas]

in the north	in het noorden	[in ət 'nōrdən]
in the south	in het zuiden	[in ət 'zœʏdən]
in the west	in het westen	[in ət 'wɛstən]
in the east	in het oosten	[in ət 'ōstən]

sea	zee (de)	[zē]
ocean	oceaan (de)	[ɔse'ān]
gulf (bay)	golf (de)	[xɔlf]
straits	straat (de)	[strāt]

continent (mainland)	continent (het)	[kɔnti'nɛnt]
island	eiland (het)	['ɛjlant]
peninsula	schiereiland (het)	['sxir·ɛjlant]
archipelago	archipel (de)	[arxipɛl]

harbor	haven (de)	['havən]
coral reef	koraalrif (het)	[kɔ'rāl·rif]
shore	oever (de)	['uvər]
coast	kust (de)	[kʉst]

flow (flood tide)	vloed (de)	['vlut]
ebb (ebb tide)	eb (de)	[ɛb]
latitude	breedtegraad (de)	['brētə·xrāt]
longitude	lengtegraad (de)	['lɛŋtə·xrāt]

| parallel | parallel (de) | [para'lɛl] |
| equator | evenaar (de) | ['ɛvənãr] |

sky	hemel (de)	['heməl]
horizon	horizon (de)	['hɔrizɔn]
atmosphere	atmosfeer (de)	[atmɔ'sfẽr]

mountain	berg (de)	[bɛrx]
summit, top	bergtop (de)	['bɛrx·tɔp]
cliff	klip (de)	[klip]
hill	heuvel (de)	['høvəl]

volcano	vulkaan (de)	[vʉl'kãn]
glacier	gletsjer (de)	['xletʃər]
waterfall	waterval (de)	['watər·val]
plain	vlakte (de)	['vlaktə]

river	rivier (de)	[ri'vir]
spring (natural source)	bron (de)	[brɔn]
bank (of river)	oever (de)	['uvər]
downstream (adv)	stroomafwaarts	[strõm·'afwãrts]
upstream (adv)	stroomopwaarts	[strõm·'ɔpwãrts]

lake	meer (het)	[mẽr]
dam	dam (de)	[dam]
canal	kanaal (het)	[ka'nãl]
swamp (marshland)	moeras (het)	[mu'ras]
ice	ijs (het)	[ɛjs]

19. Countries of the world. Part 1

Europe	Europa (het)	[ø'rɔpa]
European Union	Europese Unie (de)	[øro'pezə 'juni]
European (n)	Europeaan (de)	[ørope'ãn]
European (adj)	Europees	[øro'pẽs]

Austria	Oostenrijk (het)	['õstənrɛjk]
Great Britain	Groot-Brittannië (het)	[xrõt-bri'taniə]
England	Engeland (het)	['ɛŋɛlant]
Belgium	België (het)	['bɛlxiə]
Germany	Duitsland (het)	['dœʏtslant]

Netherlands	Nederland (het)	['nedərlant]
Holland	Holland (het)	['hɔlant]
Greece	Griekenland (het)	['xrikənlant]
Denmark	Denemarken (het)	['denəmarkən]
Ireland	Ierland (het)	['ĩrlant]

| Iceland | IJsland (het) | ['ɛjslant] |
| Spain | Spanje (het) | ['spanjə] |

Italy	Italië (het)	[i'taliə]
Cyprus	Cyprus (het)	['siprʉs]
Malta	Malta (het)	['malta]

Norway	Noorwegen (het)	['nōrwexən]
Portugal	Portugal (het)	[portʉxal]
Finland	Finland (het)	['finlant]
France	Frankrijk (het)	['frankrɛjk]
Sweden	Zweden (het)	['zwedən]

Switzerland	Zwitserland (het)	['zwitsərlant]
Scotland	Schotland (het)	['sxɔtlant]
Vatican	Vaticaanstad (de)	[vati'kān·stat]
Liechtenstein	Liechtenstein (het)	['lixtɛnstɛjn]
Luxembourg	Luxemburg (het)	['lʉksɛmbʉrx]

Monaco	Monaco (het)	[mɔ'nakɔ]
Albania	Albanië (het)	[al'baniə]
Bulgaria	Bulgarije (het)	[bʉlxa'rɛjə]
Hungary	Hongarije (het)	[hɔnxa'rɛjə]
Latvia	Letland (het)	['lɛtlant]

Lithuania	Litouwen (het)	[li'tauən]
Poland	Polen (het)	['pɔlən]
Romania	Roemenië (het)	[ru'meniə]
Serbia	Servië (het)	['sɛrviə]
Slovakia	Slowakije (het)	[slɔwa'kɛjə]

Croatia	Kroatië (het)	[krɔ'asiə]
Czech Republic	Tsjechië (het)	['tʃɛxiə]
Estonia	Estland (het)	['ɛstlant]
Bosnia and Herzegovina	Bosnië en Herzegovina (het)	['bɔsniə ən hɛrzə'xɔvina]
Macedonia (Republic of ~)	Macedonië (het)	[make'dɔniə]

Slovenia	Slovenië (het)	[slɔ'vɛniə]
Montenegro	Montenegro (het)	[mɔntə'nɛxrɔ]
Belarus	Wit-Rusland (het)	[wit-'rʉslant]
Moldova, Moldavia	Moldavië (het)	[mɔl'daviə]
Russia	Rusland (het)	['rʉslant]
Ukraine	Oekraïne (het)	[ukra'inə]

20. Countries of the world. Part 2

Asia	Azië (het)	['āzijə]
Vietnam	Vietnam (het)	[vjet'nam]
India	India (het)	['indiа]
Israel	Israël (het)	['israɛl]
China	China (het)	['ʃina]
Lebanon	Libanon (het)	['libanɔn]

Mongolia	Mongolië (het)	[mɔn'xɔliə]
Malaysia	Maleisië (het)	[ma'lɛjziə]
Pakistan	Pakistan (het)	['pakistan]
Saudi Arabia	Saoedi-Arabië (het)	[sa'udi-a'rabiə]

Thailand	Thailand (het)	['tailant]
Taiwan	Taiwan (het)	[taj'wan]
Turkey	Turkije (het)	[tʉr'kɛjə]
Japan	Japan (het)	[ja'pan]
Afghanistan	Afghanistan (het)	[af'xanistan]

Bangladesh	Bangladesh (het)	[banhla'dɛʃ]
Indonesia	Indonesië (het)	[indɔ'nɛsiə]
Jordan	Jordanië (het)	[jor'daniə]
Iraq	Irak (het)	[i'rak]
Iran	Iran (het)	[i'ran]

Cambodia	Cambodja (het)	[kam'bɔdja]
Kuwait	Koeweit (het)	[ku'wɛjt]
Laos	Laos (het)	['laɔs]
Myanmar	Myanmar (het)	['mjanmar]
Nepal	Nepal (het)	[ne'pal]

United Arab Emirates	Verenigde Arabische Emiraten	[və'rɛnixdə a'rabisə ɛmi'ratən]
Syria	Syrië (het)	['siriə]
Palestine	Palestijnse autonomie (de)	[pale'stɛjnsə autɔnɔ'mi]
South Korea	Zuid-Korea (het)	['zœʏd-kɔ'rea]
North Korea	Noord-Korea (het)	[nõrd-kɔ'rea]

United States of America	Verenigde Staten van Amerika	[və'rɛnixdə 'statən van a'merika]
Canada	Canada (het)	['kanada]
Mexico	Mexico (het)	['meksikɔ]
Argentina	Argentinië (het)	[arxɛn'tiniə]
Brazil	Brazilië (het)	[bra'ziliə]

Colombia	Colombia (het)	[kɔ'lɔmbia]
Cuba	Cuba (het)	['kʉba]
Chile	Chili (het)	['ʃili]
Venezuela	Venezuela (het)	[venəzʉ'ɛla]
Ecuador	Ecuador (het)	[ɛkwa'dɔr]

The Bahamas	Bahama's	[ba'hamas]
Panama	Panama (het)	['panama]
Egypt	Egypte (het)	[ɛ'xiptə]
Morocco	Marokko (het)	[ma'rɔkɔ]
Tunisia	Tunesië (het)	[tʉ'nɛziə]

| Kenya | Kenia (het) | ['kenia] |
| Libya | Libië (het) | ['libiə] |

South Africa	Zuid-Afrika (het)	['zœyd-'afrika]
Australia	Australië (het)	[ɔu'straliə]
New Zealand	Nieuw-Zeeland (het)	[niu-'zēlant]

21. Weather. Natural disasters

weather	weer (het)	[wēr]
weather forecast	weersvoorspelling (de)	['wērs·vōr'spɛliŋ]
temperature	temperatuur (de)	[tɛmpəra'tūr]
thermometer	thermometer (de)	['tɛrmɔmetər]
barometer	barometer (de)	['barɔ'metər]

sun	zon (de)	[zɔn]
to shine (vi)	schijnen	['sxɛjnən]
sunny (day)	zonnig	['zɔnɛx]
to come up (vi)	opgaan	['ɔpxān]
to set (vi)	ondergaan	['ɔndərxān]

rain	regen (de)	['rexən]
it's raining	het regent	[ət 'rexənt]
pouring rain	plensbui (de)	['plɛnsbœy]
rain cloud	regenwolk (de)	['rexən·wɔlk]
puddle	plas (de)	[plas]
to get wet (in rain)	nat worden	[nat 'wɔrdən]

thunderstorm	noodweer (het)	['nɔtwer]
lightning (~ strike)	bliksem (de)	['bliksəm]
to flash (vi)	flitsen	['flitsən]
thunder	donder (de)	['dɔndər]
it's thundering	het dondert	[ət 'dɔndərt]
hail	hagel (de)	['haxəl]
it's hailing	het hagelt	[ət 'haxəlt]

heat (extreme ~)	hitte (de)	['hitə]
it's hot	het is heet	[ət is hēt]
it's warm	het is warm	[ət is warm]
it's cold	het is koud	[ət is 'kaut]

fog (mist)	mist (de)	[mist]
foggy	mistig	['mistəx]
cloud	wolk (de)	[wɔlk]
cloudy (adj)	bewolkt	[bə'wɔlkt]
humidity	vochtigheid (de)	['vɔhtixhɛjt]

snow	sneeuw (de)	[snēw]
it's snowing	het sneeuwt	[ət 'snēwt]
frost (severe ~, freezing cold)	vorst (de)	[vɔrst]
below zero (adv)	onder nul	['ɔndər nʉl]
hoarfrost	rijp (de)	[rɛjp]

bad weather	onweer (het)	['ɔnwĕr]
disaster	ramp (de)	[ramp]
flood, inundation	overstroming (de)	[ɔvər'strɔmiŋ]
avalanche	lawine (de)	[la'winə]
earthquake	aardbeving (de)	['ārd·beviŋ]

tremor, quake	aardschok (de)	['ārd·sxɔk]
epicenter	epicentrum (het)	[ɛpi'sɛntrʉm]
eruption	uitbarsting (de)	['œʏtbarstiŋ]
lava	lava (de)	['lava]

tornado	windhoos (de)	['windhŏs]
twister	wervelwind (de)	['wɛrvəl·vint]
hurricane	orkaan (de)	[ɔr'kān]
tsunami	tsunami (de)	[tsʉ'nami]
cyclone	cycloon (de)	[si'klŏn]

22. Animals. Part 1

| animal | dier (het) | [dĭr] |
| predator | roofdier (het) | ['rŏf·dĭr] |

tiger	tijger (de)	['tɛjxər]
lion	leeuw (de)	[lĕw]
wolf	wolf (de)	[wɔlf]
fox	vos (de)	[vɔs]
jaguar	jaguar (de)	['jaguar]

lynx	lynx (de)	[links]
coyote	coyote (de)	[kɔ'jot]
jackal	jakhals (de)	['jakhals]
hyena	hyena (de)	[hi'ena]

squirrel	eekhoorn (de)	['ĕkhŏrn]
hedgehog	egel (de)	['exəl]
rabbit	konijn (het)	[kɔ'nɛjn]
raccoon	wasbeer (de)	['wasbĕr]

hamster	hamster (de)	['hamstər]
mole	mol (de)	[mɔl]
mouse	muis (de)	[mœʏs]
rat	rat (de)	[rat]
bat	vleermuis (de)	['vlĕr·mœʏs]

beaver	bever (de)	['bɛver]
horse	paard (het)	[pārt]
deer	hert (het)	[hɛrt]
camel	kameel (de)	[ka'mĕl]
zebra	zebra (de)	['zɛbra]
whale	walvis (de)	['walvis]

seal	rob (de)	[rɔb]
walrus	walrus (de)	['walrʉs]
dolphin	dolfijn (de)	[dɔl'fɛjn]

bear	beer (de)	[bēr]
monkey	aap (de)	[āp]
elephant	olifant (de)	['ɔlifant]
rhinoceros	neushoorn (de)	['nøshōrn]
giraffe	giraffe (de)	[xi'rafə]

hippopotamus	nijlpaard (het)	['nɛjl·pārt]
kangaroo	kangoeroe (de)	['kanxəru]
cat	poes (de)	[pus]

cow	koe (de)	[ku]
bull	stier (de)	[stir]
sheep (ewe)	schaap (het)	[sxāp]
goat	geit (de)	[xɛjt]

donkey	ezel (de)	['ezəl]
pig, hog	varken (het)	['varkən]
hen (chicken)	kip (de)	[kip]
rooster	haan (de)	[hān]

duck	eend (de)	[ēnt]
goose	gans (de)	[xans]
turkey (hen)	kalkoen (de)	[kal'kun]
sheepdog	herdershond (de)	['hɛrdərs·hont]

23. Animals. Part 2

bird	vogel (de)	['vɔxəl]
pigeon	duif (de)	['dœyf]
sparrow	mus (de)	[mʉs]
tit (great tit)	koolmees (de)	['kōlmēs]
magpie	ekster (de)	['ɛkstər]

eagle	arend (de)	['arənt]
hawk	havik (de)	['havik]
falcon	valk (de)	[valk]

swan	zwaan (de)	[zwān]
crane	kraanvogel (de)	['krān·vɔxəl]
stork	ooievaar (de)	['ōjevār]
parrot	papegaai (de)	[papə'xāj]
peacock	pauw (de)	['pau]
ostrich	struisvogel (de)	['strœys·vɔxəl]

| heron | reiger (de) | ['rɛjxər] |
| nightingale | nachtegaal (de) | ['nahtəxāl] |

swallow	zwaluw (de)	['zwaluv]
woodpecker	specht (de)	[spɛxt]
cuckoo	koekoek (de)	['kukuk]
owl	uil (de)	['œyl]

penguin	pinguïn (de)	['piŋgwin]
tuna	tonijn (de)	[tɔ'nɛjn]
trout	forel (de)	[fɔ'rɛl]
eel	paling (de)	[pa'liŋ]

shark	haai (de)	[hāj]
crab	krab (de)	[krab]
jellyfish	kwal (de)	['kwal]
octopus	octopus (de)	['ɔktɔpʉs]

starfish	zeester (de)	['zē·stər]
sea urchin	zee-egel (de)	[zē-'exəl]
seahorse	zeepaardje (het)	['zē·pārtjə]
shrimp	garnaal (de)	[xar'nāl]

snake	slang (de)	[slaŋ]
viper	adder (de)	['adər]
lizard	hagedis (de)	['haxədis]
iguana	leguaan (de)	[lexʉ'ān]
chameleon	kameleon (de)	[kamele'ɔn]
scorpion	schorpioen (de)	[sxɔrpi'un]

turtle	schildpad (de)	['sxildpat]
frog	kikker (de)	['kikər]
crocodile	krokodil (de)	[krɔkɔ'dil]

insect, bug	insect (het)	[in'sɛkt]
butterfly	vlinder (de)	['vlindər]
ant	mier (de)	[mir]
fly	vlieg (de)	[vlix]

mosquito	mug (de)	[mʉx]
beetle	kever (de)	['kevər]
bee	bij (de)	[bɛj]
spider	spin (de)	[spin]

24. Trees. Plants

tree	boom (de)	[bōm]
birch	berk (de)	[bɛrk]
oak	eik (de)	[ɛjk]
linden tree	linde (de)	['lində]
aspen	esp (de)	[ɛsp]
maple	esdoorn (de)	['ɛsdōrn]
spruce	spar (de)	[spar]

| pine | den (de) | [dɛn] |
| cedar | ceder (de) | ['seдər] |

poplar	populier (de)	[popu'lir]
rowan	lijsterbes (de)	['lɛjstərbɛs]
beech	beuk (de)	['bøk]
elm	iep (de)	[jep]

ash (tree)	es (de)	[ɛs]
chestnut	kastanje (de)	[kas'tanjə]
palm tree	palm (de)	[palm]
bush	struik (de)	['strœʏk]

mushroom	paddenstoel (de)	['padənstul]
poisonous mushroom	giftige paddenstoel (de)	['xiftixə 'padənstul]
cep (Boletus edulis)	gewoon eekhoorntjesbrood (het)	[xə'wōn ē'hontʃes·brōt]
russula	russula (de)	[ru'sula]
fly agaric	vliegenzwam (de)	['vlixən·zwam]
death cap	groene knolamaniet (de)	['xrunə 'knɔl·ama'nit]

flower	bloem (de)	[blum]
bouquet (of flowers)	boeket (het)	[bu'kɛt]
rose (flower)	roos (de)	[rōs]
tulip	tulp (de)	[tʉlp]
carnation	anjer (de)	['anjer]
camomile	kamille (de)	[ka'milə]
cactus	cactus (de)	['kaktʉs]
lily of the valley	lelietje-van-dalen (het)	['leljetʃe-van-'dalən]
snowdrop	sneeuwklokje (het)	['snēw·'klɔkjə]
water lily	waterlelie (de)	['watər·leli]

greenhouse (tropical ~)	oranjerie (de)	[ɔranʒɛ'ri]
lawn	gazon (het)	[xa'zɔn]
flowerbed	bloemperk (het)	['blum·pɛrk]

plant	plant (de)	[plant]
grass	gras (het)	[xras]
leaf	blad (het)	[blat]
petal	bloemblad (het)	['blum·blat]
stem	stengel (de)	['stɛŋəl]
young plant (shoot)	scheut (de)	[sxøt]

cereal crops	graangewassen	['xrān·xɛ'wasən]
wheat	tarwe (de)	['tarwə]
rye	rogge (de)	['rɔxə]
oats	haver (de)	['havər]

millet	gierst (de)	[xirst]
barley	gerst (de)	[xɛrst]
corn	maïs (de)	[majs]
rice	rijst (de)	[rɛjst]

25. Various useful words

balance (of situation)	balans (de)	[ba'lans]
base (basis)	basis (de)	['bazis]
beginning	begin (het)	[bə'xin]
category	categorie (de)	[katexɔ'ri]

choice	keuze (de)	['køzə]
coincidence	samenvallen (het)	['samənvalən]
comparison	vergelijking (de)	[vɛrxə'lɛjkiŋ]
degree (extent, amount)	graad (de)	[xrãt]

development	ontwikkeling (de)	[ɔnt'wikəliŋ]
difference	onderscheid (het)	['ɔndərsxɛjt]
effect (e.g., of drugs)	effect (het)	[ɛ'fɛkt]
effort (exertion)	inspanning (de)	['inspaniŋ]

element	element (het)	[ɛle'mɛnt]
example (illustration)	voorbeeld (het)	['võrbēlt]
fact	feit (het)	[fɛjt]
help	hulp (de)	[hʉlp]

ideal	ideaal (het)	[ide'ãl]
kind (sort, type)	soort (de/het)	[sõrt]
mistake, error	fout (de)	['faut]
moment	moment (het)	[mɔ'mɛnt]

obstacle	hinderpaal (de)	['hindərpãl]
part (~ of sth)	deel (het)	[dēl]
pause (break)	pauze (de)	['pauzə]
position	positie (de)	[pɔ'zitsi]

problem	probleem (het)	[prɔ'blēm]
process	proces (het)	[prɔ'sɛs]
progress	voortgang (de)	['võrtxaŋ]
property (quality)	eigenschap (de)	['ɛjxənsxap]

reaction	reactie (de)	[re'aksi]
risk	risico (het)	['rizikɔ]
secret	geheim (het)	[xə'hɛjm]
series	serie (de)	['seri]

shape (outer form)	vorm (de)	[vɔrm]
situation	situatie (de)	[sitʉ'atsi]
solution	oplossing (de)	['ɔplɔsiŋ]
standard (adj)	standaard	['standãrt]

stop (pause)	stop (de)	[stɔp]
style	stijl (de)	[stɛjl]
system	systeem (het)	[si'stēm]

table (chart)	**tabel (de)**	[ta'bɛl]
tempo, rate	**tempo (het)**	['tɛmpo]
term (word, expression)	**term (de)**	[tɛrm]
truth (e.g., moment of ~)	**waarheid (de)**	['wārhɛjt]
turn (please wait your ~)	**beurt (de)**	['børt]
urgent (adj)	**dringend**	['driŋənt]
utility (usefulness)	**nut (het)**	[nʉt]
variant (alternative)	**variant (de)**	[vari'ant]
way (means, method)	**manier (de)**	[ma'nir]
zone	**zone (de)**	['zɔnə]

26. Modifiers. Adjectives. Part 1

additional (adj)	**additioneel**	[aditsjo'nēl]
ancient (~ civilization)	**eeuwenoude**	[ēwə'naudə]
artificial (adj)	**kunstmatig**	[kʉnst'matəx]
bad (adj)	**slecht**	[slɛxt]
beautiful (person)	**mooi**	[mōj]
big (in size)	**groot**	[xrōt]
bitter (taste)	**bitter**	['bitər]
blind (sightless)	**blind**	[blint]
central (adj)	**centraal**	[sɛn'trāl]
children's (adj)	**kinder-**	['kindər]
clandestine (secret)	**ondergronds**	['ɔndər'xrɔnts]
clean (free from dirt)	**schoon**	[sxōn]
clever (smart)	**slim**	[slim]
compatible (adj)	**verenigbaar**	[və'rɛnixbār]
contented (satisfied)	**tevreden**	[təv'redən]
dangerous (adj)	**gevaarlijk**	[xe'vārlək]
dead (not alive)	**dood**	[dōt]
dense (fog, smoke)	**dicht**	[dixt]
difficult (decision)	**moeilijk**	['mujlək]
dirty (not clean)	**vuil**	[vœʏl]
easy (not difficult)	**eenvoudig**	[ēn'vaudəx]
empty (glass, room)	**leeg**	[lēx]
exact (amount)	**precies**	[prə'sis]
excellent (adj)	**uitstekend**	['œʏtstekənt]
excessive (adj)	**overdreven**	[ɔvər'drevən]
exterior (adj)	**buiten-**	['bœʏtən]
fast (quick)	**snel**	[snɛl]
fertile (land, soil)	**vruchtbaar**	['vrʉxtbār]
fragile (china, glass)	**breekbaar**	['brēkbār]
free (at no cost)	**gratis**	['xratis]

fresh (~ water)	zoet	[zut]
frozen (food)	diepvries	['dip·vris]
full (completely filled)	vol	[vɔl]
happy (adj)	gelukkig	[xə'lʉkəx]

hard (not soft)	hard	[hart]
huge (adj)	enorm	[ɛ'nɔrm]
ill (sick, unwell)	ziek	[zik]
immobile (adj)	onbeweeglijk	[ɔnbə'wɛxlək]
important (adj)	belangrijk	[bə'lanxrɛjk]

interior (adj)	binnen-	['binən]
last (e.g., ~ week)	vorig	['vɔrəx]
last (final)	laatst	[lãtst]
left (e.g., ~ side)	linker	['linkər]
legal (legitimate)	wettelijk	['wɛtələk]

light (in weight)	licht	[lixt]
liquid (fluid)	vloeibaar	['vlujbãr]
long (e.g., ~ hair)	lang	[laŋ]
loud (voice, etc.)	luid	['lœɥt]
low (voice)	zacht	[zaxt]

27. Modifiers. Adjectives. Part 2

main (principal)	hoofd-	[hõft]
matt, matte	mat	[mat]
mysterious (adj)	mysterieus	[mistɛ'røs]
narrow (street, etc.)	smal	[smal]
native (~ country)	geboorte-	[xə'bõrtə]

negative (~ response)	ontkennend	[ɔnt'kɛnənt]
new (adj)	nieuw	[niu]
next (e.g., ~ week)	volgend	['vɔlxənt]
normal (adj)	normaal	[nɔr'mãl]
not difficult (adj)	niet moeilijk	[nit 'mujlək]

obligatory (adj)	verplicht	[vər'plixt]
old (house)	oud	['aut]
open (adj)	open	['ɔpən]
opposite (adj)	tegenovergesteld	['texən·'ɔvərxəstɛlt]
ordinary (usual)	gewoon	[xə'wõn]

original (unusual)	origineel	[ɔriʒi'nẽl]
personal (adj)	persoonlijk	[pɛr'sõnlək]
polite (adj)	beleefd	[bə'lẽft]
poor (not rich)	arm	[arm]

possible (adj)	mogelijk	['mɔxələk]
principal (main)	voornaamste	[võr'nãmstə]

probable (adj)	waarschijnlijk	[wãr'sxɛjnlək]
prolonged (e.g., ~ applause)	langdurig	[laŋ'dʉrəx]
public (open to all)	openbaar	[ɔpən'bãr]

rare (adj)	zeldzaam	['zɛldzãm]
raw (uncooked)	rauw	['rau]
right (not left)	rechter	['rɛxtər]
ripe (fruit)	rijp	[rɛjp]

risky (adj)	riskant	[ris'kant]
sad (~ look)	droevig	['druvəx]
second hand (adj)	tweedehands	[twẽdə'hants]
shallow (water)	ondiep	[ɔn'dip]
sharp (blade, etc.)	scherp	[sxɛrp]

short (in length)	kort	[kɔrt]
similar (adj)	gelijkend	[xə'lɛjkənt]
small (in size)	klein	[klɛjn]
smooth (surface)	glad	[xlat]
soft (~ toys)	zacht	[zaxt]

solid (~ wall)	stevig	['stevəx]
sour (flavor, taste)	zuur	[zũr]
spacious (house, etc.)	ruim	[rœʏm]
special (adj)	speciaal	[speʃi'ãl]

straight (line, road)	recht	[rɛxt]
strong (person)	sterk	[stɛrk]
stupid (foolish)	dom	[dɔm]
superb, perfect (adj)	uitstekend	['œʏtstekənt]

sweet (sugary)	zoet	[zut]
tan (adj)	gebruind	[xə'brœʏnt]
tasty (delicious)	lekker	['lɛkər]
unclear (adj)	onduidelijk	[ɔn'dœʏdələk]

28. Verbs. Part 1

to accuse (vt)	beschuldigen	[bə'sxʉldəxən]
to agree (say yes)	instemmen	['instɛmən]
to announce (vt)	aankondigen	['ãnkɔndəxən]
to answer (vi, vt)	antwoorden	['antwõrdən]
to apologize (vi)	zich verontschuldigen	[zih vərɔnt'sxʉldəxən]

to arrive (vi)	aankomen	['ãnkɔmən]
to ask (~ oneself)	vragen	['vraxən]
to be absent	absent zijn	[ap'sɛnt zɛjn]
to be afraid	bang zijn	['baŋ zɛjn]
to be born	geboren worden	[xə'bɔrən 'wɔrdən]

to be in a hurry	zich haasten	[zix 'hāstən]
to beat (to hit)	slaan	[slān]
to begin (vt)	beginnen	[bə'xinən]
to believe (in God)	geloven	[xə'lovən]
to belong to ...	toebehoren aan ...	['tubəhɔrən ān]
to break (split into pieces)	breken	['brekən]

to build (vt)	bouwen	['bauwən]
to buy (purchase)	kopen	['kɔpən]
can (v aux)	kunnen	['kʉnən]
can (v aux)	kunnen	['kʉnən]
to cancel (call off)	afzeggen	['afzɛxən]

to catch (vt)	vangen	['vaŋən]
to change (vt)	veranderen	[və'randərən]
to check (to examine)	checken	['tʃɛkən]
to choose (select)	kiezen	['kizən]
to clean up (tidy)	schoonmaken	['sxōn·makən]

to close (vt)	sluiten	['slœɣtən]
to compare (vt)	vergelijken	[vɛrxə'lɛjkən]
to complain (vi, vt)	klagen	['klaxən]

| to confirm (vt) | bevestigen | [bə'vɛstixən] |
| to congratulate (vt) | feliciteren | [felisi'terən] |

to cook (dinner)	bereiden	[bə'rɛjdən]
to copy (vt)	kopiëren	[kɔpi'erən]
to cost (vt)	kosten	['kɔstən]

| to count (add up) | tellen | ['tɛlən] |
| to count on ... | rekenen op ... | ['rekənən ɔp] |

to create (vt)	creëren	[kre'jerən]
to cry (weep)	huilen	['hœɣlən]
to dance (vi, vt)	dansen	['dansən]

| to deceive (vi, vt) | bedriegen | [bə'drixən] |
| to decide (~ to do sth) | beslissen | [bə'slisən] |

to delete (vt)	verwijderen	[vər'wɛjdərən]
to demand (request firmly)	eisen	['ɛjsən]
to deny (vt)	ontkennen	[ɔnt'kɛnən]

| to depend on ... | afhangen van ... | ['afhaŋən van] |
| to despise (vt) | minachten | ['minaxtən] |

to die (vi)	sterven	['stɛrvən]
to dig (vt)	graven	['xravən]
to disappear (vi)	verdwijnen	[vərd'wɛjnən]
to discuss (vt)	bespreken	[bə'sprekən]
to disturb (vt)	storen	['storən]

29. Verbs. Part 2

to dive (vi)	duiken	['dœykən]
to divorce (vi)	scheiden	['sxɛjdən]
to do (vt)	doen	[dun]
to doubt (have doubts)	twijfelen	['twɛjfelən]
to drink (vi, vt)	drinken	['drinkən]

to drop (let fall)	laten vallen	['latən 'valən]
to dry (clothes, hair)	drogen	['drɔxən]
to eat (vi, vt)	eten	['etən]
to end (~ a relationship)	beëindigen	[be'ɛjndəxən]
to excuse (forgive)	excuseren	[ɛkskʉ'zerən]

to exist (vi)	existeren	[ɛksis'tɛrən]
to expect (foresee)	voorzien	[võr'zin]
to explain (vt)	verklaren	[vər'klarən]
to fall (vi)	vallen	['valən]
to fight (street fight, etc.)	vechten	['vɛxtən]
to find (vt)	vinden	['vindən]

to finish (vt)	beëindigen	[be'ɛjndəxən]
to fly (vi)	vliegen	['vlixən]
to forbid (vt)	verbieden	[vər'bidən]
to forget (vi, vt)	vergeten	[vər'xetən]
to forgive (vt)	vergeven	[vər'xevən]

to get tired	vermoeid raken	[vər'mujt 'rakən]
to give (vt)	geven	['xevən]
to go (on foot)	gaan	[xãn]
to hate (vt)	haten	['hatən]

to have (vt)	hebben	['hɛbən]
to have breakfast	ontbijten	[ɔn'bɛjtən]
to have dinner	souperen	[su'perən]
to have lunch	lunchen	['lʉnʃən]

to hear (vt)	horen	['hɔrən]
to help (vt)	helpen	['hɛlpən]
to hide (vt)	verbergen	[vər'bɛrxən]
to hope (vi, vt)	hopen	['hɔpən]
to hunt (vi, vt)	jagen	['jaxən]
to hurry (vi)	zich haasten	[zix 'hãstən]

to insist (vi, vt)	aandringen	['ãndriŋən]
to insult (vt)	beledigen	[bə'ledəxən]
to invite (vt)	uitnodigen	['œytnɔdixən]
to joke (vi)	grappen maken	['xrapən 'makən]
to keep (vt)	bewaren	[bə'warən]
to kill (vt)	doden	['dɔdən]
to know (sb)	kennen	['kɛnən]

to know (sth)	weten	['wetən]
to like (I like ...)	bevallen	[bə'valən]
to look at ...	kijken naar ...	['kɛjkən nãr]

to lose (umbrella, etc.)	verliezen	[vər'lizən]
to love (sb)	liefhebben	['lifhɛbən]
to make a mistake	zich vergissen	[zih vər'xisən]
to meet (vi, vt)	ontmoeten	[ɔnt'mutən]
to miss (school, etc.)	verzuimen	[vər'zœymən]

30. Verbs. Part 3

to obey (vi, vt)	gehoorzamen	[xə'hõrzamən]
to open (vt)	openen	['ɔpənən]
to participate (vi)	deelnemen	['dēlnemən]
to pay (vi, vt)	betalen	[bə'talən]
to permit (vt)	toestaan	['tustãn]

to play (children)	spelen	['spelən]
to pray (vi, vt)	bidden	['bidən]
to promise (vt)	beloven	[bə'lovən]
to propose (vt)	voorstellen	['võrstɛlən]
to prove (vt)	bewijzen	[bə'wɛjzən]
to read (vi, vt)	lezen	['lezən]

to receive (vt)	ontvangen	[ɔnt'faŋən]
to rent (sth from sb)	huren	['hʉrən]
to repeat (say again)	herhalen	[hɛr'halən]
to reserve, to book	reserveren	[rezɛr'verən]
to run (vi)	rennen	['renən]

to save (rescue)	redden	['rɛdən]
to say (~ thank you)	zeggen	['zexən]
to see (vt)	zien	[zin]
to sell (vt)	verkopen	[vɛr'kɔpən]
to send (vt)	sturen	['stʉrən]
to shoot (vi)	schieten	['sxitən]

to shout (vi)	schreeuwen	['sxrēwən]
to show (vt)	tonen	['tɔnən]
to sign (document)	ondertekenen	['ɔndər'tekənən]
to sing (vi)	fluiten, zingen	['flœytən], ['ziŋən]
to sit down (vi)	gaan zitten	[xãn 'zitən]

to smile (vi)	glimlachen	['xlimlahən]
to speak (vi, vt)	spreken	['sprekən]
to steal (money, etc.)	stelen	['stelən]
to stop (please ~ calling me)	ophouden	['ɔphaudən]
to study (vt)	studeren	[stʉ'derən]

to swim (vi)	zwemmen	['zwɛmən]
to take (vt)	nemen	['nemən]
to talk to …	spreken met …	['sprekən mɛt]
to tell (story, joke)	vertellen	[vər'tɛlən]
to thank (vt)	danken	['dankən]
to think (vi, vt)	denken	['dɛnkən]

to translate (vt)	vertalen	[vər'talən]
to trust (vt)	vertrouwen	[vər'trauwən]
to try (attempt)	proberen	[prɔ'berən]
to turn (e.g., ~ left)	afslaan	['afslān]
to turn off	uitdoen	['œɤtdun]

to turn on	aandoen	['āndun]
to understand (vt)	begrijpen	[bə'xrɛjpən]
to wait (vt)	wachten	['waxtən]
to want (wish, desire)	willen	['wilən]
to work (vi)	werken	['wɛrkən]
to write (vt)	schrijven	['sxrɛjvən]

www.ingramcontent.com/pod-product-compliance
Lightning Source LLC
Chambersburg PA
CBHW060025050426
42448CB00012B/2869